C000217767

Casemate Short History

ANCIENT EGYPTIAN WARFARE

TACTICS, WEAPONS AND IDEOLOGY OF THE PHARAOHS

Ian Shaw

CASEMATE

Oxford & Philadelphia

Published in Great Britain and
the United States of America in 2019 by
CASEMATE PUBLISHERS
The Old Music Hall, 106–108 Cowley Road, Oxford OX4 1JE, UK
1950 Lawrence Road, Havertown, PA 19083, USA

© Casemate Publishers 2019

Paperback Edition: ISBN 978-1-61200-7250
Digital Edition: ISBN 978-1-61200-7267

All rights reserved. No part of this book may be reproduced or transmitted in
any form or by any means, electronic or mechanical including photocopying,
recording or by any information storage and retrieval system, without
permission from the publisher in writing.

A CIP record for this book is available from the British Library

Printed in the Czech Republic by FINIDR s.r.o.

All line drawings and photographs are Ian Shaw's unless stated otherwise.

Typeset in India for Casemate Publishing Services.
www.casematepublishingservices.com

For a complete list of Casemate titles, please contact:

CASEMATE PUBLISHERS (UK)
Telephone (01865) 241249
Email: casemate-uk@casematepublishers.co.uk
www.casematepublishers.co.uk

CASEMATE PUBLISHERS (US)
Telephone (610) 853-9131
Fax (610) 853-9146
Email: casemate@casematepublishers.com
www.casematepublishers.com

CONTENTS

Part of a row of Asiatic captives, depicted in the Temple of Amun at Karnak, taking the form of foreign place-names inscribed inside cartouche-style city-wall ideograms, each symbolizing a defeated Syro-Palestinian city state, 18th Dynasty, c.1550–1400 BC.

INTRODUCTION

A WIDE VARIETY OF APPROACHES HAVE been taken to the study of Egyptian warfare, ranging from the analysis of battle tactics to the cataloguing of types of physical injury. The excellent preservation of military equipment, such as bows, axes and chariots, has provided the basis for numerous detailed discussions of the changing nature of Egyptian military technology. However, most analyses of ancient Egyptian warfare have tended to focus on a variety of more abstract areas such as political history, military strategy, symbolism, and the topography and ethnography of the ancient world, often steering away from the practical questions of life, death and survival on the battlefield. This situation is exacerbated by the inclination of many of the ancient textual and artistic sources to present battles not as historical events but as aspects of the myth and symbolism of the king and the gods.

Researchers have only rarely focused on the practical experiences of the individual Egyptian soldiers on the battlefield. Chapter 4 addresses this issue, discussing firstly the 'official' Egyptian view of battle and then the much more difficult topic of the roles, attitudes and physical and mental experiences of individual Egyptian soldiers. Since much of the analysis is based on pictorial and textual evidence, the discussion inevitably deals as much with the aims and purpose of the documents and images themselves as with the elusive underlying reality of Egyptian battle.

Typically, many aspects of daily life that were portrayed on the walls of Egyptian tombs – such as agriculture or craftwork – have survived to some extent in the archaeological record at the sites of ancient towns and villages. Battle scenes are very occasionally portrayed in tombs, and quite frequently portrayed on the walls of New Kingdom temples (see Chapter 3), but relatively few corresponding archaeological traces have survived. The battlefield is among the most transient and ephemeral of man-made features, and even the most famous battles of medieval and post-medieval Europe have often proved difficult to locate and explore precisely through archaeology. In Egypt, although the arid climate has helped to preserve both battle-scarred human remains and weaponry, the actual landscapes in which conflicts took place have proved much more difficult to identify.

The earliest anthropological evidence for battle in Egypt takes the form of a Palaeolithic mass-grave of hunter-gatherers (mostly killed by flint-tipped arrows) at the site of Jebel Sahaba, in modern Sudan. Nine thousand years later, at the end of the 3rd millennium BC, at least sixty Middle Kingdom soldiers were buried in a mass-grave near the tomb of the 11th-Dynasty ruler Nebhepetra Mentuhotep II (c.2055–2004 BC) in western Thebes, many having died from severe head wounds probably incurred in the course of siege warfare. Physical evidence of this type is an invaluable means of verifying and complementing the details of the surviving textual and pictorial descriptions of Egyptian battle. These anthropological and medical data are discussed in Chapter 4.

In the late Predynastic and the early pharaonic period (c.3200–2900 BC), the main sources for Egyptian warfare take the form of images and ideogrammatic 'proto-texts' that are mostly carved on ceremonial and votive artefacts, such as knife-handles, cosmetic palettes, mace-heads and bone and ivory labels (see Chapter 1). The reliefs on these artefacts are characterized by constantly repeated motifs: the king smiting foreigners, the siege and capture of fortified settlements, the binding and execution of prisoners, and the offering of the spoils of war to the gods. These have been interpreted in a variety of ways by scholars, but the general consensus is that they may often refer to generic aspects of warfare and hostility rather than to actual battles that took place at specific times and places.

Later visual and textual sources include tomb paintings and massive temple reliefs depicting campaigns and battles, as well as victory stelae and the funerary 'biographies' of such key military personalities as the 11th-Dynasty general Intef (c.2030 BC) and the early New Kingdom admiral Ahmose, son of Ibana (c.1550–1500 BC). All of these were relatively public displays of the Egyptian view of battle; just as the works of Classical historians and biographers were written with particular aims and readers in mind, so the pharaonic descriptions of war and battle had their own agenda, and any study must be sensitive not only to content but also to the nuances of literary and artistic forms. If the paintings and reliefs depicting Egyptian battles are to be understood properly, their physical and cultural contexts must also be taken into account. There are clearly two major sources of information: a number of private tombs, at Deshasha, Saqqara, Beni Hasan and Thebes, dating to the late Old Kingdom and Middle Kingdom (c.2345–1782 BC) and the temple reliefs of the Ramesside period (c.1293–1070 BC) at Thebes and numerous sites in Nubia, of which the most important group are those devoted to the battle of Qadesh (see Chapter 3). This battle took place in the fifth year of the reign of Ramesses II (c.1274 BC). Tremendous publicity was given to the Qadesh conflict, which was depicted on no fewer than five of Ramesses II's most important temples (Luxor, Karnak, Abu Simbel, Abydos and the Ramesseum), while the literary account has also been preserved on three papyri. Although the scale of the commemoration implies that it was intended to be regarded as a high point in Ramesses' reign, it seems likely that it was at best a case of stalemate, and at worst a severe setback to Ramesses' empire-building.

The reliefs and inscriptions relating to New Kingdom warfare were mostly parts of the decoration of tombs or cult and mortuary temples; they were therefore inextricably linked with the funerary and religious cults themselves. The common placement of battle reliefs in full view on the exterior walls of temples seems to make it clear that at least one of the aims of these monuments was to express ideology relating to power and violence, particularly in relation to the elite culture surrounding the Egyptian king. Indeed, it is worth noting that, whereas in modern times warfare and battle are primarily regarded as destructive and abhorrent aspects of life and society, in ancient Egypt such violence was regarded not only as an essential element of kingship but also as a positive and stabilizing aspect of the role played by the king in ensuring the presence and maintenance of *maat* (a very specific Egyptian concept relating to truth and harmony) in society. The ideological purpose of the pharaoh was to maintain the stability of the universe; he was thus obliged to fight battles on behalf of the gods and then to bring back prisoners and booty as votive offerings for their temples.

It is possible to compare Egyptian weaponry, tactics and strategy with those that appear to have been employed by their Near Eastern neighbours, to get a sense of what might be described as the 'knowledge network' of warfare in the Late Bronze Age (see Chapter 6). To what extent did the great empires of the Late Bronze Age differ from one another in their attitudes and approaches to battle, and to what extent can we see their approaches 'converging' during this period as people, ideas and artefacts flowed back and forth in the form of booty, prisoners of war and elite diplomatic exchange?

A closely related issue is the set of possible mechanisms by which war affects technology. This is a question of cause and effect: do innovations in military technology provide significant benefits in terms of the production of commodities and services during peacetime, and can war therefore be regarded as an agent of technical progress? Some scholars have argued that, although military needs served at times as 'focusing devices', weapons were more frequently dependent on developments in civilian technology rather than acting as sources of inspiration for the latter. There is no doubt that, as in other periods and places, we are dealing with a very complex web of social and technological factors.

Chapter 7 deals with the surprisingly detailed information that we have for naval warfare in Egypt and the Near East from the Early Bronze Age to the Iron Age. The Nile was always the principal means of transport in ancient Egypt, and the sailing and construction of boats can be traced back to the papyrus rafts of the Predynastic period. Ancient Egyptian depictions of sea battles range from the carved relief images of boats on a prehistoric ivory knife-handle from Gebel el-Arak to the temple reliefs of the 20th-Dynasty ruler Ramesses III showing what appears to be a specific battle against the so-called Sea Peoples in *c.*1174 BC.

We cannot study warfare without also examining ancient attempts to *avoid* conflict – the surviving records of 'diplomatic' contact and early peace treaties are surprisingly rich, even as far back as the Bronze Age. The most important textual sources for Egyptian involvement in international diplomacy are restricted to only a few decades in the 14th century BC, but they present a vivid view of surprisingly complex interactions between the elite groups of Late Bronze Age Near East. These sources comprise an important cache of clay cuneiform tablets discovered at the New Kingdom Egyptian city site of Amarna (c.1350–1320 BC). The 'Amarna Letters' are discussed in Chapter 8, alongside other evidence for the dynamic and ever-changing picture of alliances, enmities and peace treaties that characterized Egypt's links with the outside world.

The vast majority of the documents in the Amarna archive are items of diplomatic correspondence between Egypt and either the great powers in Western Asia, such as Babylonia and Assyria, or the vassal states of Syria-Palestine. The apparent parlous state of the Egyptian empire under the so-called 'heretic king' Akhenaten (c.1352–1336 BC) is poignantly documented in the increasingly desperate pleas for assistance from Syro-Palestinian cities under siege. As well as giving insights into the political conditions of the time, the letters also shed light on trade relations, diplomatic marriage and the values of particular commodities such as glass, gold and the newly introduced iron, while the various forms of address employed in the letters indicate the standing of the writers vis-à-vis the Egyptian court.

Ancient Egyptian visual and textual sources may frequently focus on the cosmological and religious aspects of warfare, but this should not blind us to the real practicalities of Egyptian contacts with other states and rulers in the ancient Near East and the east Mediterranean region.

_c._700/500,000–10,000 BP PALAEOLITHIC
_c._5300–3000 BC PREDYNASTIC PERIOD

_c._3200–3000 BC	Naqada III/'Dynasty 0'
_c._3000 BC	Reign of Narmer

3000–2686 BC EARLY DYNASTIC PERIOD

3000–2890 BC	1st Dynasty
2890–2686 BC	2nd Dynasty

2686–2125 BC OLD KINGDOM

2686–2613 BC	3rd Dynasty
2613–2494 BC	4th Dynasty
2494–2345 BC	5th Dynasty
2345–2181 BC	6th Dynasty
2181–2125 BC	7th and 8th Dynasties

2160–2055 BC FIRST INTERMEDIATE PERIOD

2160–2025 BC	9th and 10th Dynasties
2125–2055 BC	11th Dynasty (Thebes only)

2055–1650 BC MIDDLE KINGDOM

2055–1985 BC	11th Dynasty (all Egypt)
1985–1795 BC	12th Dynasty
1795–after 1650 BC	13th Dynasty
1750–1650 BC	14th Dynasty

1650–1550 BC SECOND INTERMEDIATE PERIOD

1650–1550 BC	15th Dynasty (Hyksos)
1650–1580 BC	16th Dynasty
_c._1580–1550 BC	17th Dynasty

1550–1069 BC NEW KINGDOM

1550–1295 BC	18th Dynasty
1525–1504 BC	Reign of Amenhotep I (Djeserkara)
1504–1492 BC	Reign of Thutmose I (Aakheperkara)
1492–1479 BC	Reign of Thutmose II (Aakheperenra)
1479–1425 BC	Reign of Thutmose III (Menkheperra)
_c._1457 BC	Battle of Megiddo
1427–1400 BC	Reign of Amenhotep II (Aakheperura)
1400–1390 BC	Reign of Thutmose IV (Menkheperura)

1390–1352 BC	Reign of Amenhotep III (Nebmaatra)
	Reign of Amenhotep IV/Akhenaten
1336–1327 BC	Reign of Tutankhamun (Nebkheperura)
1323–1295 BC	Reign of Horemheb (Djeserkheperura)
1295–1069 BC	**RAMESSIDE PERIOD**
1295–1186 BC	19th Dynasty
1294–1279 BC	Reign of Seti I
1279–1213 BC	Reign of Ramesses II
c.1274 BC	Battle of Qadesh
1213–1203 BC	Reign of Merenptah
1186–1069 BC	20th Dynasty
1184–1153 BC	Reign of Ramesses III
1099–1069 BC	Reign of Ramesses XI
1069–664 BC	**THIRD INTERMEDIATE PERIOD**
1069–945 BC	21st Dynasty
945–715 BC	22nd Dynasty
818–715 BC	23rd Dynasty
727–715 BC	24th Dynasty
747–656 BC	25th Dynasty
747–716 BC	Reign of Piankhi (Menkheperra)
664–332 BC	**LATE PERIOD**
664–525 BC	26th Dynasty
525–404 BC	27th Dynasty (1st Persian period)
404–399 BC	28th Dynasty
399–380 BC	29th Dynasty
380–343 BC	30th Dynasty
362–360 BC	Reign of Teos (Irma atenra)
343–332 BC	2nd Persian period
332–32 BC	**PTOLEMAIC PERIOD**
30 BC–AD 311	**ROMAN PERIOD**

Based on Shaw, I. 2000. (ed.) *Oxford History of Ancient Egypt.* Oxford

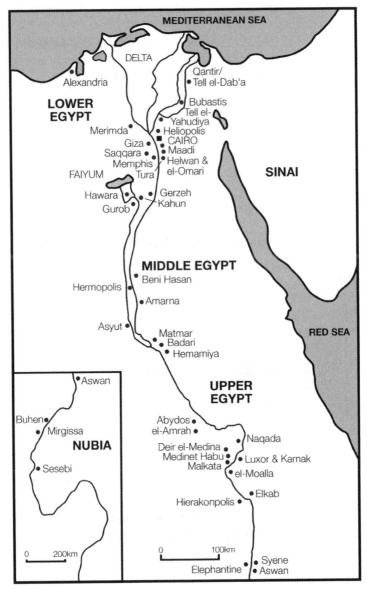

Map of Egypt, showing the main towns and cities, including the main Predynastic centres of power (Hierakonpolis, Naqada and Abydos/This). (Paul Vyse)

CHAPTER 1

INTERPRETING THE EVIDENCE FOR EGYPTIAN WARFARE

WHAT IS THE REAL STARTING POINT for our evidence of warfare in ancient Egypt? The introduction has already mentioned very early evidence for the possible effects of battle, in the form of the numerous fatally injured individuals buried at the Palaeolithic site of Jebel Sahaba. For many millennia after Jebel Sahaba, the archaeological record is comparatively silent in terms of warfare, until we reach the 4th millennium BC, and the emergence of a sequence of Predynastic cultures in Egypt and Nubia. In the last few centuries of the prehistoric period, Egypt began to change from a very fragmented collection of farms and villages into a highly centralized and sophisticated state. We can tell from the gradually increasing depictions of battles that the late Predynastic was probably a time of growing conflict within Egypt, as more and more local chiefs and their villages grew stronger and expanded. With each local victory the political geography of Egypt was gradually being altered until, on the brink of unification into a single state (*c*.3000 BC), it must have consisted of a series of large regions rather like the provinces or nomes of the pharaonic period, each probably vying for supremacy.

Eventually there seem to have been three main areas (Naqada, Hierakonpolis and This/Abydos), all of which were struggling for power in the late Predynastic period – this epoch is sometimes described as the 'Protodynastic', lasting from about 3200 to 3000 BC. The three competing regions were all in Upper (i.e. southern) Egypt, and it is possible that the earlier emergence of kingdoms in Upper Egypt, as opposed to Lower Egypt, might have been determined at least partly by physical geography. In Upper Egypt the relatively narrow confines of the Nile Valley may have created the kind of political and demographic 'pressure-cooker' that was needed to encourage the growth of city-states, whereas the settlements in the north of Egypt (the Delta) were scattered over a very much wider area of fertile land, and therefore perhaps less prone to military conflict and resultant political unification. It is also possible that the strength and precocity of Upper Egyptian states might have been tied in with their exploitation of gold mines and trade routes in the Eastern Desert.

Hierakonpolis: scenes of violent conflict

The ancient city of Nekhen – or Hierakonpolis, as it was later known in Ptolemaic and Roman times – was the cult centre of the hawk-god Horus. The town and its surrounding cemeteries may well have been the first significant urban centre in the Nile Valley, situated 50 miles south of Luxor. The region is almost 15 hectares, comprising the pharaonic town and temple near the flood plain, and various areas of earlier settlement, cemeteries and rock carvings in the desert to the west. It reached its peak during the late Predynastic and Early Dynastic periods (*c.*4000–2649 BC). The most substantial surviving part of the Early Dynastic city is known as Kom el-Gemuwia. Archaeological research at Kom el-Gemuwia and other parts of Hierakonpolis began in 1898, with the excavations of the British Egyptologists James Quibell and Frederick Green in a temple founded in the late 4th millennium BC, when Egyptian civilization was just emerging from prehistory.

It was in the 1899 season at Hierakonpolis that Green discovered a completely unique thing – a Predynastic tomb that contained painted images on its walls, some of which appear to portray aspects of the violence that characterized the period. Much of the mud-plaster covering the walls of Tomb 100 was damaged, but the southwestern wall had survived better than the rest, and was decorated with paintings executed mainly in black, grey and brown on an ochre background, which have been dated stylistically to the mid-4th millennium BC; there were also some traces of paintings surviving on a free-standing wall in the centre of the grave. These are still the only wall-paintings to have been found in any Egyptian Predynastic grave. The southwestern wall is dominated by images of a group of six huge boats, interspersed with smaller scenes apparently representing aspects of hunting and battle. Like the decoration on late Predynastic painted pottery vessels (which they closely resemble), the images in Tomb 100 can be interpreted in numerous different ways. One possibility is that these are simply faithful depictions of life along the Nile Valley, including boats, religious images and hunting and trapping scenes in the desert, but it is also possible that they comprise early icons relating to military power and elite ideology. One image shows a male figure standing between two animals (probably lions), with two pairs of warriors apparently engaged in hand-to-hand combat nearby. Among the hunting images is a scene that seems to show a gazelle caught by a lasso, as well as dogs chasing oryxes. Unlike dynastic Egyptian art (but similar to the art on Predynastic pottery), the images in the tomb are not arranged into distinct spatial 'registers' or levels. Instead, they are spread apparently randomly across the surface of the wall, without any sense of deliberate arrangement or naturalistic organization. Some of the later examples of this kind of art, however, such as the 'Narmer Palette' (Egyptian Museum, Cairo; discussed in more detail later) do show some use of a 'register' system to arrange the decoration into rows.

Although both the tomb's architecture and some of the images in the paintings are comparable with the elite Dynasty 0 tombs in Cemetery T at Naqada (c.3100 BC), the many grave goods found inside Tomb 100 have been conclusively shown to date to the Naqada IIc period, some two or three centuries earlier.

The mace as an early royal symbol of power One of the scenes in the painted decoration of Tomb 100 shows a warrior threatening three prisoners with a mace. In the 1990s, an even earlier example of the motif, showing a tall figure smiting three crouching captives, was found painted on a pottery vessel excavated from the Predynastic tomb U-239 at Abydos (dated to c.3500 BC). This classic icon of the smiting pharaoh was to retain its significance for thousands of years, appearing in a variety of religious and artistic contexts.

The mace was a basic hand-held offensive weapon, comprising a stone head attached to a shaft made of wood (or sometimes ivory or horn). Many mace-heads have been excavated from Predynastic and Early Dynastic cemeteries. The earliest examples, dating to the Naqada I period (c.4000–3500 BC), were discoid. The discovery of an early Predynastic clay model mace-head at Mostagedda suggests that some may have been intended as ritualistic or symbolic objects.

In the Naqada II period (c.3500–3200 BC), the discoid form was largely superseded by the classic pear-shaped head, as well as a narrow, pointed form that may have been introduced from Western Asia. As discussed above, by the late Predynastic period both ceremonial palettes and mace-heads had become part of the iconography of power surrounding the emerging kingship and the associated elite group. Few maces of any kind have been found after the end of the Early Dynastic period, suggesting that by then the weapon was no longer used as a standard weapon of war and survived purely as an elite ritual item.

The image of the triumphant king brandishing a mace had already become an enduring image of kingship by the time the Narmer Palette was carved, and the mace-head itself had become a vehicle for royal propaganda. The mace was associated symbolically with the healthy eye of the god Horus, whose epithets included the phrase 'lord of the mace, smiting down his foes'.

The iconography of warfare at the beginning of Egyptian history

A number of images of early battle and conquest were carved onto a distinctive set of early elite artefacts primarily comprising votive palettes, mace-heads and ivory knife-handles from late prehistory and the first two dynasties (c.3300–2700 BC). These items of so-called 'mobiliary art' (i.e. art that can be carried around) have usually been found either in early temples or among the funerary equipment in graves. They have often been used as evidence to create theories concerning the emergence and unification of the early pharaonic state. The items that date towards the end of the Predynastic and the beginning of the historical period (c.3300–3000 BC) tend to be decorated with images increasingly related to hunting and battle. It should be noted that hunting had become a relatively small aspect of the subsistence pattern in the late Predynastic; therefore, scenes of hunting portrayed at this late date have become increasingly regarded as the ceremonial acts of elite groups, rather than simply images relating to the acquisition of food.

Although early Egyptologists tended to try to make quite literal interpretations of images that seemed to portray battle, presenting them as early historical narratives of acts of conquest that may actually have happened at specific points in time, it has become more common to regard them now as representations relating to ideas that were important to an emerging elite. Many of these actions relate to the Egyptians' subtle fusion of political and religious systems, in which the role of the pharaoh was to maintain the stability of the universe; he was thus obliged to fight battles on behalf of the gods and then to bring back prisoners and booty as votive offerings for their temples.

Several significant palettes and mace-heads were found in an early Egyptian temple at Hierakonpolis, including fragments of a large limestone ritual pear-shaped mace-head that bears signs spelling out the royal name Narmer (c.3000 BC). The scenes carved on this ritual weapon appear to portray early rituals associated with kingship, one of which is interpreted as the first known version of the ritual known as *khaty-bity*: 'the appearance of the King of Lower Egypt'. In addition to the Narmer mace-head, fragments were found of another limestone mace-head of a similar type (now in the Ashmolean Museum, Oxford), this time decorated with raised relief scenes, including a man wearing the Upper Egyptian white crown. This individual is the largest figure on the mace-head and appears to be identified by the ideogram hovering in front of him as King Scorpion, who might have been Narmer's predecessor on the throne.

The figure of Scorpion is grasping a large hoe, while a servant holds out to him a basket, perhaps to catch the earth he is removing from the ground. That he and his servant are standing immediately beside some kind of water-course has led to suggestions that he is ritually excavating an irrigation canal with the help of attendants. As a result of this interpretation, which is widely held but not necessarily conclusively proven, the Scorpion mace-head has frequently been used as a crucial piece of evidence in the hypothesis that the Egyptian state, and its characteristic monarchical style of government, emerged through the control of water by an elite group. The presence of a row of so-called *rekhyt*-birds (lapwings, which, in Egyptian art, usually symbolized subject peoples or enemies) hanging by their necks on ropes suspended from a series of standards in the top register of the mace-head, are an indication that warfare and death were part of the backdrop even to early hydrology.

One researcher, Nicholas Millet, argued that the purpose of the images and texts on the palettes and mace-heads of the late 4th and early 3rd millennia BC was not to describe historical events in themselves but simply to commemorate individual years in early kings' reigns. He pointed out that the scenes on the Narmer mace-head resemble the brief lists of rituals given for each year of the kings' reigns on the Palermo Stone (a 5th-Dynasty basalt stele bearing royal annals).

The Gebel el-Arak knife-handle

Some elite tombs dating between Naqada IId and the 1st Dynasty include elaborately carved ceremonial knives with ivory handles as part of the funerary assemblages. These decorated knife-handles constitute a significant source on late Predynastic culture, and they share some of their imagery with the roughly contemporary votive/ceremonial palettes and mace-heads. Most handles tend to be decorated with carved scenes of rows of animals, as well as more complex iconography involving imaginary creatures. One of these ripple-flaked flint knives, said to have been discovered somewhere in the vicinity of Gebel el-Arak (on the east bank of the Nile near the modern city of Nag Hammadi) and dated to the Naqada III period, is carved with much more complex decoration, involving humans as well as animals.

This so-called Gebel el-Arak knife-handle is evidently an important example of the aggressive imagery dating from the crucial formative phase of Egyptian civilization. The knife (now in the Louvre) was not found through legitimate excavation but acquired on the antiquities market by the French Egyptologist Georges Bénédite in 1914. Its original archaeological context is therefore uncertain: it has been suggested that it may actually derive from Abydos, but at least one scholar has argued that it is so unique that it may be a forgery. The high quality of the artefact, both in its materials and craftsmanship, would suggest that it derives from the funerary assemblage of an elite individual (or, alternatively, was perhaps a votive item in a temple).

The handle of the knife, carved from a single hippopotamus tusk, is decorated on both sides with finely engraved bas-relief representations in a style that is considered more Syrian or Mesopotamian than Egyptian. One face of the handle bears representations of a variety of wild animals and two domesticated dogs. Above them are two lions held apart by a bearded man wearing a long robe and unusual headgear. Both the costume and the distinctive motif of a man between two beasts are Mesopotamian in origin.

The other side of the handle is carved with scenes of hand-to-hand fighting (using axes, clubs and knives) between foot-soldiers in the upper part. The lower section bears images of boats, perhaps comprising an early sea battle (see Chapter 7 for further discussion of this): both the maritime scene and the human 'hero' figure between lions are similar to those depicted in the 'decorated tomb' at Hierakonpolis. The wild animals and battle scenes could be interpreted as iconographic indications of the widespread conflict that preceded the establishment of a unified Egyptian state.

The Battlefield Palette

An early ceremonial palette bearing images that appear to portray a battlefield has survived in the form of three fragments now spread across three collections: the British Museum, London; the Ashmolean Museum, Oxford; and the Köfler-Truniger collection,

*The two decorated faces of the Gebel el-Arak knife handle, Naqada III period,
c.3200–3000 BC.*

Lucerne. It is said to have been acquired in the early 20th century at
the site of Abydos.

The largest of the three fragments of delicately carved greywacke (a
greenish-grey slate-like stone), comprising the whole of the lower section
of the palette, is in the British Museum. On one side of the piece, a pair
of long-necked gazelles are shown grazing on a central date-palm. A
bird with a hooked beak (on the Oxford fragment) is shown behind
the head of one of the gazelles. The other side is decorated with a scene
showing both prisoners and dead warriors, the latter being devoured by
vultures, ravens and (in the centre of the palette) a lion. It is possible that
the lion is intended to represent the king (given that much later texts
and imagery make this metaphorical link), but it is also possible that
the lion, like the vultures, is only intended to be seen as a wild animal
preying on the corpses.

At the top right of the main fragment, a bent and trussed prisoner
is shown in front of a figure wearing a long decorated cloak. It is
faintly possible that part of an image in front of the prisoner may be
a very early version of the 'land' hieroglyphic ideogram, surmounted
by papyrus plants, thus perhaps indicating his place of origin. The

Oxford fragment, at the top left, portrays two further prisoners, whose arms are tied behind their backs and 'held' by military standards bearing images of an ibis and a falcon. Judging from the Lucerne fragment, the decoration higher up on the palette seems to have consisted more depictions of dead warriors. On the right-hand edge of the Oxford fragment, in front of the two captives, is part of the standard circular area surrounded by a raised ridge, in which cosmetic pigments would have been crushed, had this been used an actual palette (rather than being a an elaborate, ceremonial, votive item). The dead and injured are all shown as bearded, curly-haired, and circumcised, and it has been suggested that these may be early depictions of defeated *tjehenu* (a term usually thought to refer to Bronze Age groups in the area now occupied by modern Libya).

The Narmer Palette

Royal smiting scene on the verso of the Protodynastic Narmer palette, Egyptian Museum, Cairo, c.3000 BC.

In 1898 the British Egyptologists Quibell and Green uncovered a beautifully carved shield-shaped slab of greywacke in the ruins of an early temple at the Upper Egyptian site of Hierakonpolis. This Protodynastic votive palette bears carved low-relief decoration on both faces. It is usually dated to the final century of the 4th millennium BC. In the top register on the front of the palette, the artist has carved the striding bearded figure of an early Egyptian ruler, probably identified as a man called Narmer, judging by the hieroglyphs both in front of him and in the so-called *serekh* frame (a rectangular panel probably representing the entrance to an early royal palace) in the centre of the top of the palette, between two cow's heads representing the early goddess Bat. The king is shown wearing the so-called Red Crown, which eventually became connected with the control of Lower Egypt (but whether it had yet developed this association in Naqada I or in Narmer's time is uncertain), carrying a mace and a flail, and wearing a tunic tied over his left shoulder, with a bull's tail hanging from the waist. King Narmer is taking part in a procession with six other people, including two high officials and four smaller standard-bearers, all of whom are evidently reviewing the decapitated bodies of ten of their enemies, who are laid out on the far right, each with his head and severed penis between his legs, presumably in the aftermath of a battle or ritual slaughter. On the other side of the palette (or 'verso', see illustration) is a much larger, muscular striding figure of Narmer, this time shown wearing the conical White Crown of Upper Egypt along with the same tunic tied over his left shoulder and the bull's tail hanging from his waist, as well as fringes ending in cows' heads. The king is gripping the hair of a captive who has two ideograms floating to the right of his head, perhaps giving name, title or place of origin. In front of the king, and above the captive, the falcon-god Horus hovers, holding a schematically rendered captive by a rope attached to the man's nose. In the lower section of this side of the palette, two further bearded human figures (similar to the captive above) are shown – these are sprawling, as if dead. Each of these two men has an ideogram carved by his head, one clearly indicating a rectangular walled town, and the other more difficult to interpret, but, according to Yigael Yadin, perhaps representing a desert animal trap, and therefore possibly indicating the defeat of a nomadic group, in which case the neighbouring figure might be intended to represent a conquered urban group.

Most scholars regard the scenes on the Narmer Palette as highly iconographic and symbolic. The visual appearance and the very complex content of the Narmer Palette's decoration have been the subject of constant discussion ever since its discovery. The style of the images and the identification of the king as Narmer demonstrate that it was created at the end of the 4th millennium BC, when many of the most distinctive elements of Egyptian culture were emerging.

The Narmer Label In 1993, while sifting through spoil heaps left behind both by the ancient conversion of the Abydos tombs into shrines and by 19th- and 20th-century excavators, a German team found an almost complete ivory label decorated with images similar to some of those on the Narmer Palette. These types of labels (usually made from wood, bone or ivory) were found both in the Early Dynastic royal tombs and the late Predynastic elite burials of Cemetery U, and gave information concerning items placed in the tomb.

The upper line of inscription on the Narmer label closely resembles the smiting scene on the Narmer Palette, except that the image is transformed into a form of hieroglyphic sentence comprising the name Narmer, which appears twice, once on the right-hand side in a *serekh* frame and once in the middle of the inscription but this time with two arms having been added to the *nar* hieroglyph (the catfish sign) so that it can wield a mace in one hand and grasp a bearded foreigner in the other. The foreigner sprouts papyrus plants from his head (like the schematic man held prisoner by the Horus falcon on the Narmer Palette) and has a small 'bowl' hieroglyph to his left. At the top left a vulture hovers over a rectangle perhaps representing the royal palace, with a falcon-topped standard in front of it. This is very plausibly interpreted as the sentence 'Smiting the *tjehenu* marshland people by Horus Narmer, celebration (of victory) of the palace'. Since it presumably identifies a specific year in the king's reign, as the other labels do, it seems likely that it identifies the same year as the scenes depicted on the Narmer Palette.

In addition, a tiny ivory cylinder bearing the name of Narmer was found at Hierakonpolis and probably also belongs to the same year in Narmer's reign, since it shows the catfish smiting three rows of foreign captives identified with the same word *tjehenu* (usually translated as 'Libyans'). Taken together, the label, cylinder and palette of Narmer seem to be all decorated with information describing a particular year in the king's reign. Günter Dreyer, the German Egyptologist who excavated the label, has therefore argued that the label indicates that King Narmer's defeat of northerners/Libyans was an actual historical event. This assessment, however, seems rather premature – an alternative assumption would be that we have three records of the same event, but are no closer to knowing whether it was a genuine military triumph.

The prime universal importance of the acquisition of foreign captives can be demonstrated by comparing the main smiting scene on the Narmer Palette with a similar motif found in Early Dynastic Mesopotamia, on the Victory Stele of Eannatum (also known as the 'Stele of the Vultures', *c.*2560 BC), which portrays the god Ningirsu wielding a mace over a group of naked enemies trapped in a net. Similarly, among the ancient Maya of Mesoamerica it is argued that the main cause of warfare was neither territorial expansion nor economic gain but the need to obtain sacrificial victims and thus a tendency to capture enemies alive rather than killing them.

It is likely, however, that, even at this early stage in Egyptian history, the political and economic motivations for warfare – the defence of borders and the acquisition of valuable land, livestock, natural resources and slaves – were being masked, to some extent, by layers of religion and ritual, providing both moral justification and a 'universal' framework. The tradition of religious justification for war was maintained throughout the pharaonic period, and even turned against the Egyptians themselves in the case of the Victory Stele of the 25th-Dynasty Nubian pharaoh Piankhi (*c.*734 BC), in which he justified his conquest of Egypt in terms of a crusade on behalf of the Egyptian god Amun.

The tendency for the earliest Egyptian images and inscriptions to oversimplify the motivations for warfare and the nature of battle can largely be explained by the fact that such objects as palettes and ceremonial mace-heads were never intended to provide historical accounts of battle. The motifs on these votive gifts were designed to function within the emerging cults of the king and the various 'local' and 'national' deities with which he associated himself, and the battlefield was merely a convenient artistic context for the depiction of ritual acts and universal truths. The king is often portrayed in such bestial forms as a bull or a lion to emphasize his symbolic role as the protector of Egypt from the forces of chaos and evil.

Battle scenes in tombs of the Old Kingdom and First Intermediate Period

Images of battle are extremely rare in the tombs of both Old and New Kingdom high officials, and it was only for a short period in the 6th to 12th Dynasties that a number of officials and provincial governors appear to have regarded warfare as sufficiently important to have battle-scenes portrayed in their tombs. It is uncertain precisely what may be deduced from these battle paintings. On a broad historical level, two major historical factors seem to be at work: first the breakdown of order and stability at the end of the Old Kingdom, resulting in widespread conflict between the different provinces, and secondly the fact that the Old Kingdom rulers' *ad hoc* system of recruiting groups of untrained young men as soldiers was superseded during the First Intermediate Period by the creation of small professional armies under the command of local governors, which would eventually form the nucleus of a national army in the Middle Kingdom.

Part of the earliest Old Kingdom battle scene, showing archers drawing their bows, has survived in the form of a fragment of relief from the 4th-Dynasty royal mortuary complex of Khufu (*c*.2589–2566 BC). The only other known royal depiction of battle in the Old Kingdom is from the funerary causeway of the 5th-Dynasty pharaoh Unas at Saqqara (*c*.2375–2345 BC), where the reliefs include fragments of a confrontation between an Asiatic soldier and Egyptians armed with daggers, bows and arrows. This theme of Egyptians attacking Asiatics is repeated in two 5th-Dynasty tombs belonging to non-royal individuals (that of Inti at Deshasha, and that of Kaemheset, at Saqqara), where the painted wall decoration includes portrayal of the use of sophisticated siege technology (see Chapter 2). Both of these tombs appear to show sieges of Asiatic fortified towns, suggesting that Egypt was already launching military campaigns into the Levant during the Old Kingdom. From at least the late Old Kingdom onwards, the depiction of Egyptian battles became more detailed and narrative-based, rather than simply expressing 'eternal truths' about the kingship, as may have been the case with the scenes on Protodynastic palettes, mace-heads and knife-handles discussed above.

The tomb of Setka at Aswan, dating either to the late Old Kingdom or to the First Intermediate Period, contains some human images that appear to represent Nubian archers operating within the Egyptian army, or at least within a local army at the southern border, controlled by Setka, whose titles included 'governor' and 'overseer of foreign lands'. The row of seven soldiers, one holding an animal-skin shield and the rest either using or holding bows and arrows, appear to be in combat (indeed one was probably injured) but the identity of the opposing army is not known. These Nubian soldiers wear distinctive feathers on their heads, and their coloured kilts are similar to leather examples found in C-Group burials in Nubia.

Some of the surviving First Intermediate Period funerary paintings and texts, such as those in the tomb of the local warlord Ankhtifi at el-Moalla (*c.*2100 BC), make it clear that this era was characterized by greater conflict between the individual regions of Egypt. Provincial governors continued to play a more military role in the early Middle Kingdom, and on an artistic level there must also have been a greater desire or necessity to celebrate military achievements in Middle Kingdom private tombs. The existence of the precedents described above in the late Old Kingdom tombs of Inti and Kaemheset may suggest that funerary art was already reflecting social and political change as the Old Kingdom went into decline. After the end of the Old Kingdom, military capabilities both at local and national levels probably became just as crucial as they had been a thousand years earlier, in the build up towards the 1st Dynasty and the unification of the first Egyptian state. Of course one of the many outstanding questions concerning the political history of the First Intermediate Period is whether the fragmentation at the end of the Old Kingdom can really be compared with the warring city states of the late Predynastic period.

It has been suggested that the two main events in Ankhtifi's political career were his attempts to pacify and reorganize the nome of Edfu, and a military expedition against a coalition of the Theban and Koptite nomes, who appear to have refused to give battle. This quote from his lengthy funerary 'biography' on the walls of his tomb at el-Moalla gives some sense of the growth of local 'kinglets' in the absence of a strong central ruler:

> I sailed downstream with my strong and trustworthy troops and moored on the west bank of the Theban nome...and my trustworthy troops searched for battle throughout the west of the Theban nome, but nobody dared to come out through fear of them. Then I sailed downstream again and moored on the east bank of the Theban nome... and his [Ankhtifi's opponent's?] walls were besieged since he had locked the gates through fear of these strong and trustworthy troops. They became a search party looking for battle throughout the west and

the east of the Theban nome, but nobody dared to come out through fear of them.

Ankhtifi makes repeated reference to his army, and one of the walls of his tomb shows some of the soldiers, perhaps hunting, with their bows and arrows, accompanied by hounds. The soldiers are holding bunches of arrows and long self-bows. Apart from shields, their only bodily

Ideogram of an Egyptian soldier holding a throw-stick and adze, from the tomb of Ankhtifi, el-Moalla, c.2150–2050 BC.

protection is a band of webbing across the shoulders and chest, since body armour was not introduced until the New Kingdom, and even then primarily for elite members of the army. The texts in Ankhtify's tomb also include an intriguing insight into First Intermediate Period weaponry, in the form of the army (*mšꜥ*) hieroglyphic determinative sign used in his biography. The usual ideogram of a soldier with bow and arrows is replaced, in Ankhtifi's inscriptions, by a figure holding a throw-stick and possibly an adze, or sometimes two adzes. A possible explanation would be that First Intermediate Period warfare may have been largely concerned with besieging towns, and that the adzes might therefore have been for undermining walls, as in the images of besieged towns on the late Predynastic Cities Palette, which are shown being attacked with hoes.

Four other First Intermediate Period tombs, each located at Asyut, contain images of soldiers and battle, all probably dating to around the time of the 11th-Dynasty ruler Mentuhotep II. The first of these, the tomb of Iti-ibi, includes a fragmentary scene that appears to show one Egyptian soldier using two long sticks with curved ends to strike another man (perhaps a soldier), who also seems to be Egyptian. Since no other parts of the scene have survived, it is difficult to be sure whether this is a scene of punishment or battle, but it may perhaps be another vignette of civil war.

The second example, the tomb of Iti-ibi-ikr, who held the title 'Overseer of Troops of the Entire Thirteenth Nome', has a

Two soldiers and accompanying dogs, from the private army of the First Intermediate Period provincial ruler Ankhtifi, portrayed in his tomb at el-Moalla, c.2150–2050 BC.

fragmentary set of surviving images on its north wall, at the base of which are scenes including soldiers armed with bows and battle axes. The men are largely shown marching but one can be seen to be releasing an arrow from his bow. The lack of any visible enemy suggests that the aim of the images was simply to portray the troops commanded by Iti-ibi-ikr rather than to show a scene of battle. The two other tombs at Asyut both include painted depictions of rows of soldiers holding shields and long-handled, convex-bladed battle axes.

Wooden models of soldiers and weaponry

As well as the two-dimensional scenes of battles depicted on the walls of tombs, another category of evidence for warfare takes the form of painted wooden models, dating mainly to the First Intermediate Period and Middle Kingdom. Among the most important sources for the study of Egyptian weapons in the early Middle Kingdom are two wooden models (Cairo, Egyptian Museum) from the tomb of Mesehti, a provincial governor at Asyut in the 11th Dynasty. Forty Egyptian spearmen and forty Nubian archers are reproduced in faithful detail, showing the typical costume and arms of the common soldier. The Egyptian spearmen are wearing short linen kilts and carry a shield in the left hand and a spear, with a long leaf-shaped bronze blade, in the right. Each shield is painted with a different design imitating the mottled markings of cowhide. It has been pointed out that Mesehti's soldiers show strong similarities with the troops depicted in the tomb of Iti-ibi-ikr.

The Nubian archers are dressed somewhat differently, in more elaborate green and red loincloths, probably made from leather rather than linen. They carry their wooden recurved bows in one hand and bunches of arrows in the other (like the soldiers portrayed in the tomb of Ankhtifi). Another tomb at Asyut, belonging to a 12th-Dynasty nobleman called Nakht, included a whole replica armoury, including full-size spears (of a very similar type to those in Mesehti's model), two cylindrical spear-cases, two bows and arrows and a shield (Cairo, Egyptian Museum and Paris, Louvre).

Scenes of Middle Kingdom battle in tombs and temples at Beni Hasan and Thebes

Two Middle Kingdom cemeteries include rock tombs in which the wall decoration incorporates scenes of warfare: firstly Beni Hasan, in Middle Egypt, and secondly, Thebes, in the south. There are four rock-tombs containing battle scenes at Beni Hasan, and all of these are located at the bottom of the eastern wall of the main chamber of the funerary chapel.

Along with the depictions of funerary offerings and such activities as dancing, hunting, fishing or agriculture, these Middle Kingdom battle scenes seem to have formed part of a visual summary of many aspects of the life of the deceased. The battles depicted might have been a combination of smaller skirmishes or might never have taken place, just as the deceased may never actually have speared fish from a papyrus skiff (another common funerary scene). Indeed it has been pointed out that the scenes of siege warfare at Beni Hasan resemble one another sufficiently closely to suggest that they are all fictional, or at least that only the earliest of them might depict a unique historical event.

The Beni Hasan scenes – like some of the First Intermediate Period texts and images described above – appear to document

Wooden funerary model depicting Egyptian warriors, from the tomb of Mesehti at Asyut, l. 168.5cm, w. 62.5cm c.2025 BC. (Egyptian Museum, Cairo)

civil war between rival factions of Egyptians. This suggests that the content of funerary art was responding to some extent to historical events rather than endlessly repeating the same generalized motifs. The onset of civil war and the professionalization of the army would both have conspired temporarily to raise the profile of military activities in the lives of some of the provincial governors, thus necessitating the depictions of battles on the walls of their tombs, alongside their more peaceful activities.

There are, however, also some scenes of Egyptian conflict with Asiatics in the Middle Kingdom. Both the reliefs from King Nebhepetra Mentuhotep II's mortuary temple at Deir el-Bahari and the images portrayed in the nearby tomb of his general Intef appear to portray siege warfare against Asiatic foes (see Chapter 2). In addition, there are a few fragments of battle scenes between Egyptians and Asiatics that decorated the funerary causeways of the 12th-Dynasty rulers Senusret I and III, at Lisht and Dahshur respectively.

Many of the surviving images and texts of warfare in Old–Middle Kingdom private tombs relate in some way to the siege and capture of individual towns or fortresses, implying perhaps that this – rather than pitched battle in the open – was the most common form of battle during these periods. As the next chapter demonstrates, the topic of fortresses and siege warfare is well attested in the archaeology, texts and visual imagery of Egypt from the Neolithic through to the Iron Age.

CHAPTER 2

FORTRESSES AND SIEGE WARFARE

THE EARLIEST SURVIVING EGYPTIAN FORTIFICATIONS WERE built to protect towns rather than to defend frontiers. Apart from the hieroglyphic symbols for 'city' (*niwt*), 'enclosure' (*ḥwt*), and 'palace with battlements' (*ꜥḥ*) which are plans of circular and rectangular enclosure walls, detailed representations of fortified towns have survived from the earliest times in Egypt. Probably the first evidence for an Egyptian fortress is a Predynastic ceramic model of a building, discovered by Flinders Petrie at Abadiya, which appears to show two men peering over a crenellated wall (Ashmolean Museum, Oxford). Memphis, the capital of Egypt for most of its history, was said to have been founded in the form of a fortress called the White Wall by Menes, the first king of Egypt.

Only the lower section of the so-called Cities Palette (also known as the Tjehenu or Libyan Palette) has survived. The provenance of this fragment of a shield-shaped greywacke ceremonial palette is unknown, and it is now in the Egyptian Museum, Cairo. The reverse side of the palette shows two rows of walled cities or fortifications (four in the upper register and three in the lower), each of which is being attacked by an animal or animal standard using a hoe. It seems likely that the hoes were being used to physically undermine the mud-brick fortifications, as in the battle scene in the Old Kingdom tomb of Khaemhesy. Within each fortification icon is a number of symbols, which have been interpreted as the names of towns; because one of these is a heron, perhaps representing the town of Buto in the northwestern Delta, it is thought possible that these may show northern cities under siege, perhaps by a southern ruler. These images of fortified places under siege are similar in appearance to the fortified enclosure that is portrayed in the process of demolition by a bull, at the base of the front of the Narmer Palette.

Siege warfare portrayed in tombs

Two private tombs in the late Old Kingdom contained scenes portraying siege warfare: the 5th-Dynasty tombs of Inti at Deshasha, and Kaemheset at Saqqara. A crucial issue with these images, as with the Protodynastic material discussed above, concerns the extent to which we can regard them as depictions of real factual events.

The tomb of Inti incorporates a depiction of a battle in front of an Asiatic fortress (probably a fortified settlement in southern Palestine), which can be broken down into three sections from top to bottom: in the upper register, a squad of Egyptian archers are assembling; in the two middle registers the Egyptian infantry armed with battle-axes are engaged in hand-to-hand combat with the defenders, some of whom are pierced by arrows. In the lowest register the Asiatics are being marched off into captivity along with their wives and children, while to the right a ladder is used to ascend the wall of the fortress, the foot of which is being mined by two soldiers with picks. In terms of the human reactions to battle, the events shown on five registers in the interior of the fortress are perhaps the most revealing, including scenes of defenders apparently being struck by their wives (perhaps for cowardice), while in the top register a man is breaking his bow before the gaze of his family – the archetypal gesture of surrender. The importance of warfare to Inti's career as a royal official is indicated by his title *imy-r mnww nswt* ('overseer of royal fortresses'), as well as him being a local governor, or nomarch.

In the tomb of Kaemheset (which is probably roughly contemporary with that of Inti, although there has been considerable debate concerning its date) there is a portrayal of what appears to be a scaling ladder on wheels being used in the siege, as well as a small cameo scene of a man driving his sheep and cattle into a wood, presumably to prevent their capture by the Egyptians. In other respects, the scene in Kaemheset's tomb closely resembles that in Inti's, leading some researchers to argue that both might be based on original prototype imagery perhaps deriving from artists working for the elite group based in the capital, Memphis. This suggestion would of course also affect

Battle scene, probably including the use of a mobile siege tower, 11th-Dynasty tomb of Intef at Thebes, c.2055–2004 BC.

our views on any possibly historicity of these Old Kingdom images of battle, perhaps suggesting that they belong to a generic repertoire rather than being portrayals of actual historical events. Although there has, in the past, been some debate as to whether the inhabitants of the besieged town are Asiatic or Egyptian, recent reanalysis of the paintings in Kaemheset's tomb suggests that the women are wearing Asiatic dress similar to that portrayed in the mortuary complex of Sahura.

One further early private tomb contains images of siege warfare that appear to show a Syro-Palestinian setting. This is the 11th-Dynasty tomb of Intef, who was contemporary with King Nebhepetra Mentuhotep II. His tomb (TT386), in the Asasif region of western Thebes, was decorated with texts and images reflecting his military career as an *imy-r mš ͨ* (usually translated as 'overseer or troops' or general), including a portrayal of what appears to be the successful siege of an Asiatic fortress, and the subsequent butchering and capture of its Palestinian inhabitants. Notable aspects of this scene include the presence of Nubian archers within the Egyptian army (wearing their distinctive costume, including a form of sporran), and the use of a wooden siege tower, pushed up against the fortified town wall, and therefore allowing the Egyptian soldiers to enter the besieged town. The fragments of painted battle scenes from the mortuary temple of Intef's ruler, Mentuhotep II (now spread across the collections of the British Museum, Royal Ontario Museum and the Metropolitan in New York), may even portray the same siege scene. Two of the fragments show parts of a scene of soldiers ascending a siege ladder with enemies (Asiatics or possibly fellow-Egyptians) falling around them, pierced by arrows.

The paintings in the tombs of two 11th-Dynasty provincial governors, Khety and Baqt III at Beni Hasan (numbered BH15 and

Siege scene in the tomb of Khety at Beni Hassan, including the possible use of an early battering ram c.2055–2004 BC.

BH17 respectively), include depictions of soldiers laying siege to fortified towns in Egypt, no doubt directly reflecting the civil wars that took place in Middle and Upper Egypt in the late First Intermediate Period. These Egyptian fortifications appear to have consisted of high walls, crenellated at the top and strengthened with a slight batter at the base. The numerous wounds found on the heads of sixty 11th-Dynasty soldiers (buried in a mass-grave near the mortuary complex of Mentuhotep II at Deir el-Bahari, see Chapter 4) perhaps bear witness to the fatal consequences of attempting to storm such battlements.

The siege scene in the tomb of Khety is characterized by a combination of archers and infantry in the attack on a fortress but with the addition of a group of men protected by a portable roofed structure apparently advancing towards the fortress with a pole (perhaps an early battering ram). Interestingly, however, the scene is in this instance a purely military one. Unlike the Asiatic sieges in the tombs of Inti, Kaemheset and Intef, there is no apparent pictorial reference to the panic, surrender and enslavement of the occupants, suggesting perhaps that the civilian consequences of wars between Egyptians were less lethal than the reprisals taken against Asiatics.

The defence of Egypt's frontiers

The question of Egyptian fortresses, as opposed to fortified towns, is very closely connected with that of frontiers. The traditional borders of Egypt comprised the Western Desert, the Sinai Desert, the Mediterranean coast and the First Nile Cataract at Aswan. Such natural physical barriers were sufficient to protect the Egyptians from outside interference for the many centuries during which their distinctive civilization developed. Later in the Dynastic Period these natural borders helped to maintain Egypt's independence during periods of relative weakness. Since, however, the pharaoh's titulary described him as the ruler of the entire known world, the political boundaries of Egypt were theoretically infinite. In times of strength and prosperity certain rulers, such as Senusret I and Thutmose III, declared their intention to 'extend the borders' (swsḫ tꜣšw) of Egypt.

In practice the furthest extent of the Egyptian empire – achieved during the reign of Thutmose III in the 18th Dynasty – was marked by the Euphrates in the northeast and the Kurgus boundary stelae (between the Fourth and Fifth Nile Cataracts) in the south. The northeastern, northwestern and southern borders of Egypt were more or less fortified from the Middle Kingdom onwards. From at least the reign of Amenemhat I (c.1985–1956 BC) the eastern Delta was protected by a string of fortresses, known as the Walls of the Prince (inbw ḥkꜣ). These were intended to prevent invasion along the coastal route from the Levant, which was known as the 'Ways of Horus' during the Middle Kingdom. At about the same time a fortress seems to have been established in the Wadi Natrun, defending the western Delta from the Libyans. The western and eastern Delta defences were well maintained throughout the 2nd millennium BC, including New Kingdom fortresses and garrisons on the Delta borders, such as Zawiyet Umm el-Rakham in the west and Tell Abu Sefa (Sile), Tell el-Hebua, Tell Borg and Tell el-Maskhuta (Pithom) in the east.

In the south of Egypt, the border with Kush (Lower Nubia) was traditionally marked by the town of Elephantine, naturally defended by its island location and surrounded by a thick defensive wall. The original name of the settlement around the First Cataract was Swn, meaning 'trade' (from which the modern name Aswan derives); this place name reflects the more commercial nature of the southern border, representing opportunities for profitable economic activities rather than the threat of invasion. Because the First Cataract represented an obstacle to shipping (despite an attempt by the Old Kingdom ruler Merenra to cut a canal), all trade goods had to be transported along the bank. This crucial land route to the east of the Nile, between Aswan and the region of Philae, was protected by a huge mud-brick wall, almost 7.5 kilometres (4.6 miles) long, probably built principally in the 12th Dynasty. The land route at the Second Cataract (in the region of Semna) was defended by a similar fortification.

The Nubian fortresses

In the Old Kingdom (c.2686–2160 BC) the Egyptian presence in Nubia seems to have principally consisted of a succession of trading and mining expeditions, peacefully exploiting valuable animal and mineral resources. Probably the earliest surviving permanently occupied Egyptian outpost in Nubia was a small Old Kingdom settlement located about 250 metres northeast of the Middle Kingdom fortress at Buhen, near the Second Cataract. It was excavated in 1962–64 by Bryan Emery, revealing a sandstone and mud-brick town covering an area of $c.124,000$ m^2, and protected by a large, crudely built stone fortification. This site has been dated to the 4th and 5th Dynasties (and possibly as early as the 2nd Dynasty) and was apparently devoted primarily to the smelting of copper. The settlement included standard Egyptian 4th- and 5th-Dynasty pottery, as well as mud-sealings of similar date. However, it also included Nubian A-Group pottery, suggesting that, prior to the construction of the buildings occupied by the Egyptian mining/ smelting community, there was some kind of earlier settlement populated by local indigenous people at around the Naqada III/ Protodynastic period in Egyptian terms.

During the Middle Kingdom, the Egyptians embarked on a programme of military expansion into Nubia, bolstering their position with a long chain of fortresses between modern Aswan and the region of the Second Cataract. These heavily fortified settlements, located at the most vulnerable points in the trade route from the south, were simultaneously both military outposts and customs stations. Most of them have now vanished irretrievably beneath the waters of Lake Nasser since the raising of the Aswan High Dam in 1971. Fortunately, however, the rescue excavations of the Nubian Salvage Campaign in 1959–69 have provided a great deal of information concerning this unique group of sites. Virtually all of the forts were built, mainly in mud brick, over a period of about 125 years (c.1956–1831 BC), from the reign of Senusret I to that of his great-grandson Senusret III. A large cluster of eleven fortresses was established by Senusret III in the area of the Second Cataract, each positioned to control the flow of traffic northwards at points where the Nile was difficult to negotiate. The southernmost of these (Semna West, Kumma, Uronarti and Semna South) were located about 50 kilometres (30 miles) south of the Second Cataract, around the narrowest gorge in the whole course of the Nile, marking the final frontier in the 12th Dynasty.

Fortress design

All of the Second Cataract forts had similar internal plans, consisting of a grid-plan of specialized zones for store-rooms, workshops, barracks and officers' houses. These various quarters were linked and intersected by a network of well-constructed streets and drains,

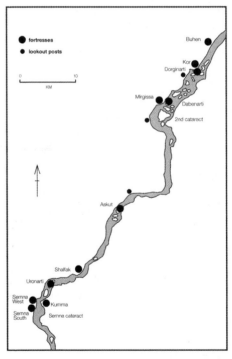

Map of Nubia showing the locations of Middle Kingdom fortresses. (Paul Vyse)

often built of stone. The whole community was usually encircled by a street around the inside of the walls (known as a *pomoerium*), allowing troops speedy and convenient access to the battlements. Most of the forts were linked with the Nile by covered or walled stairways. The Semna South fortress was provided with a granite-lined tunnel, passing under the river-side defences, which appears to have been intended to supply an alternative source of fresh water, presumably in the event of a siege.

Although the general uniformity of the Middle Kingdom forts' ground-plans suggests that they were probably designed by only one or two architects, they show fascinating variations in response to the local topography. Whereas the two largest sites, Buhen and Mirgissa, were simply rectangular structures (as were all five of the surviving forts north of the Second Cataract group), the rest, mostly located further to the south, had idiosyncratic shapes dictated by the terrain. The fort at Semna West, for instance, was built in an L-shape to conform with the rocky hill on which it stood. At Uronarti, an island near Semna,

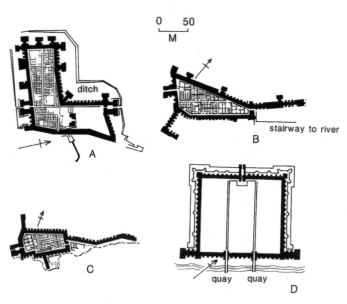

Plans of four Middle Kingdom fortresses: (A) Semna West, (B) Uronarti, (C) Shalfak, and (D) Buhen. (Paul Vyse)

the fort was triangular and the northern side was more heavily fortified with huge towers, since the flatter terrain to the north made attacks from that direction more dangerous. In addition two long spur walls stretched away from the main Uronarti fort to the south and northeast, so that the whole irregular island was afforded maximum protection. Spur walls were used in the same way at Shalfak and Askut.

The 'plains fortresses'

By far the most elaborate of the Nubian fortresses were Mirgissa, Buhen and Aniba – the three so-called 'plains fortresses'. The largest of these, Mirgissa, is now securely identified with the fort named as Iken in Senusret III's Semna stelae (see below). It actually consisted of a whole complex of smaller sites, including the fortress itself (covering 40,000 square metres), a large, unfortified settlement area, several cemeteries, an extensive quayside and a mud-lined slipway, more than two kilometres long (so that boats could be dragged along the bank, thus avoiding the Kabuka rapids). These two latter factors suggest that Mirgissa was not only a garrison but also a depot for the warehousing of trade goods. One side of the main Mirgissa fortress (facing the Western Desert) was felt to be more vulnerable to attack and was therefore given an additional outer wall. Inside the fort the excavations revealed an armoury of spears, arrows and shields at various stages in the manufacturing process.

A pit near the main fortress at Mirgissa contained hundreds of potsherds and clay figurines (and in one case a human skull), most of which were inscribed with so-called 'execration texts' (curses against enemies), as well as four inscribed limestone statues of captives, and a human body that had perhaps been deliberately decapitated as a sacrifice. All of this material perhaps comprised magical defences to back up the physical military fortifications. About a kilometre to the east of Mirgissa was also the small, apparently unfinished island-fortress of Dabenarti.

The Buhen fortress was located at the northern end of the Second Cataract region, so that the Nile was from then on easily navigable up to the First Cataract at Aswan. It was well situated to act as a large depot for trade goods from the Middle Kingdom until the late New Kingdom. The grandiose defences included an outer enclosure wall over 700 metres (2,250 feet) long and 4 metres (13 feet) thick. The wall was strengthened at intervals by 32 semi-circular bastions; this outer defence was probably intended to protect the builders while the complicated inner fortifications were being constructed. The western wall had five large towers as well as a huge central tower which functioned as the main gateway to the site; this entrance (known as the 'barbican') was gradually strengthened over the years, developing into a huge tower, measuring 47 by 30 metres (150 by 100 feet), with two baffle entrances, double wooden doors and even a drawbridge on rollers. The inner walls of the fort, 5 metres (16 feet) thick and at least 11 metres (36 feet) high, also had square towers at the corners and bastions at five-metre intervals, each provided with triple loopholes through which archers could fire on attackers. Both outer and inner defences were surrounded by ditches following the outline of the walls, with salients at the points where towers or bastions projected from the outer surface. Although Buhen was undoubtedly the most sophisticated Middle Kingdom fortress in Nubia, most of its elements – such as loopholes, berms, counterscarps, glacis and bastions – also appear to varying degrees in the other 12th-Dynasty forts.

The Semna gorge fortresses

The Semna gorge was the narrowest part of the Nile Valley. It was here, at this strategic location, that Senusret III built a cluster of five mud-brick fortresses: Semna West, Kumma, Semna South, Shalfak and Uronarti. These fortifications effectively blocked the river in this area, and a dam may perhaps also have been built, leaving only a small channel for the passage of boats.

Lake Nasser, created by the completion of the Aswan High Dam in 1971, has engulfed most of these fortresses, with only Shalfak and Uronarti remaining as islands in the floods. The rectangular Kumma fortress, the L-shaped Semna West fortress (on the opposite bank) and the much smaller square fortress of Semna South were investigated by the American archaeologist George Reisner in 1924 and 1928. Semna West and Kumma also included the remains of temples, houses and cemeteries from the New Kingdom, which

The outer enclosure wall of the Buhen fortress. (UNESCO Connected Open Heritage Project)

would have been roughly contemporary with such New Kingdom Egyptian settlements in Lower Nubia as Amara West and Sesebi-Sudla, when the Second Cataract region had arguably become part of an Egyptian 'empire', rather than simply a frontier zone.

Uronarti fortress, situated on an island to the north of the main Semna Cataract, was originally excavated in the late 1920s. The site has been re-examined since 2012 by a joint mission of Brown University and the Austrian Academy of Sciences; the recent work has revealed a 12th-Dynasty extra-mural settlement, perhaps occupied by local Nubian C-group people. The main area of the Middle Kingdom fortress is *c.*140 metres in length, and the outer walls are *c.*5 metres thick, and probably originally *c.*10 metres in height. A spur wall extends to the north for *c.*220 metres, its two main purposes presumably having been to prevent anyone from crossing the island at that point and to provide a series of lookout posts. The principal entrance, a fortified gateway, is located in the south wall, with a steep slope in front of making it very difficult to attack. Inside the fortress, the entire area is filled with buildings – the northern set being made up mostly of granaries, while the south comprised a mixture of administrative and residential structures (as well as animal pens). All of these buildings were linked and intersected by a system of streets, which also ran along the interiors of the outer walls; the major artery, running along the fortress's main axis, was paved with roughly hewn local stone. Excavated artefacts included weighing scales, suggesting that this site, along with Semna West, may have played a role in processing the gold extracted south of the Second Cataract. Wooden tokens in the shape of loaves have also been found, probably exchanged for bread or grain rations during the fort's Middle Kingdom occupation. Like Semna West and Kumma, the site continued in use into the New Kingdom, when the fortress was extended using sandstone blocks, and a small temple was built by Thutmose III.

Military bread-ration tokens from the fortress of Uronarti, made from wood with decoration in painted plaster, late 12th Dynasty, c.1900–1800 BC, diameter of round tokens c.13cm. (© 2019 Museum of Fine Arts Boston)

The Shalfak fortress is situated on the west bank of the Nile, on the edge of a high rocky outcrop. Its main occupation area measures about 80 × 49 metres (making it the smallest of the Middle Kingdom fortresses, apart from the unfinished one at Dabenarti), and, as at the other fortresses, the thickness of the walls was around 5 metres. Three spur walls increased the area that it was able to defend, particularly the northeastern one, which ran for about 115 metres. About a quarter of the internal space is taken up by granaries, and the rest mainly comprises residential buildings. The main fortified gateway is at the western end of the fort, but there is also a smaller entrance to the east.

Shalfak is currently being excavated by a team from University College London. One of their most surprising discoveries relates to the visual appearance of Middle Kingdom military architecture – not only were the outer fortification walls at Shalfak found to have been painted yellow and white, but a painters' workplace was found, including lumps of pigment and large quantities of yellow and white paint. The mud-brick walls of the fortress also include frequent use of halfa grass and sedge matting, as well as acacia logs, inserted between the courses of mud brick, probably to minimize shrinkage, cracking and collapse.

Frontier texts

By the New Kingdom (and presumably also in the Middle Kingdom) the Second Cataract forts were united under the command of Buhen, the traditional centre of Egyptian operations in Nubia. A series of lookout posts, consisting of clusters of rough stone huts (often accompanied by graffiti carved in the cliff-face) at strategic high points along the banks, helped to maintain strong communication links between the forts. Some aspects of the political and economic roles of these fortresses are clarified by the texts of two so-called 'boundary stelae' set up by Senusret III at Semna West fortress in the eighth and sixteenth years of his reign. There are three stelae altogether, including a virtually identical duplicate of the year 16 stele, excavated at Uronarti fortress.

The year 8 stele (now in Berlin) is inscribed with a short hieroglyphic text, and includes a clear definition of the Nubian frontier: 'Southern boundary, made in the year 8, under the majesty of the King of Upper and Lower Egypt, Khakaura Senusret III who is given life forever and ever; in order to ensure that no Nubian [nhsy – literally 'southerner'] should cross it, by water or by land, with a ship, or any herds of the Nubians; except a Nubian who may come to trade in Iken [the fortress of Mirgissa] or with a commission. Every good thing shall be done with them, but without allowing a ship of the Nubians to pass by Heh [perhaps the ancient name of Semna West fortress], going downstream, forever.'

The two copies of the year 16 boundary stele (the Semna West one now being in Berlin and the Uronarti one in Khartoum) were each inscribed with a much longer text than the year 8 one. Rather than stressing the minutiae of trading regulations, the year 16 stelae focus much more on anti-Nubian rhetoric and the concept of moving the border further to the south through military action. In the first part of the text it is stated that 'the king made his southern boundary at Heh [Semna West fortress?]: I have made my boundary further south than my fathers, I have added to what was bequeathed me'.

The main reason for the Second Cataract fortresses was evidently not the protection of Egypt's southern border, for they would have been easily outflanked by invaders passing along the desert on either side. Nor were the forts simply designed to subjugate Lower Nubia. Instead, the year 8 Semna West stele in particular seems to indicate that the string of fortresses functioned primarily as a means of enforcing the Egyptian king's monopoly on trade goods (especially gold, ivory, animals and slaves) emanating from African peoples further to the south, through Upper Nubia, which was known to the Egyptians of the Old Kingdom as Yam.

A set of papyri found in a white plastered box in a 13th-Dynasty shaft tomb underneath the mortuary temple of Ramesses II on the Theban west bank at Luxor included one that is now known as the Ramesseum Onomasticon (Papyrus Berlin 10495). This papyrus includes a list of Egyptian fortresses in Nubia, evidently enumerating them from south to north. The names of seventeen forts are given, and most appear fairly aggressive in nature, such as 'Subduing the Setiu-Nubians' (Semna South fortresss), 'Warding off the Bows' (Kumma), 'Repressing the Medjay' (Serra East), 'Destroying the Nubians' (Askut), 'Repelling the Inuntiu-Nubians' (Uronarti), and 'Curbing the Foreign Countries' (Shalfak). It has been suggested that, as with some other Egyptian place-names, each of these may be an abbreviation of an original name that included the name of the ruler who founded the fortresses: Senusret III. Thus the full name of Semna South, for instance, might have been 'Senusret III subdues the Setiu-Nubians'. A few others are less bellicose and perhaps to be interpreted more as simple political statements – thus Faras was called 'Embracing the Two Lands' (possibly referring to Nubia being absorbed into Egypt's territory), and Semna West is simply 'Khakaura (Senusret III) is Powerful'. Some appear to have been named after an indigenous local toponym, e.g. Iken (Mirgissa), Miam (Aniba), Baki (Kubban) and Buhen.

The plastered box from the Middle Kingdom tomb also contained fragments of papyri bearing a set of despatches sent from the Semna West fortress. Papyrus Ramesseum C, now in the British Museum, dates to the reign of Amenemhat III (*c.*1831–1786 BC) and contains fascinating evidence of the close watch kept on the movements of foreigners in the vicinity of the Second Cataract. Highly detailed information, including much that may seem trivial in modern terms, was evidently conveyed between the fortresses and presumably also back to the military headquarters in Thebes, judging from the small sample of correspondence that survives. Two further fragments of papyrus from the box (labelled together as Papyrus Ramesseum 18) seem to be orders sent from the Middle Kingdom military headquarters at Thebes. These newly translated texts back up previous information that suggested that the Vizier's Office at Thebes was communicating directly with individual fortresses. One letter informs the fortresses of Elephantine and Kubban that they are about to be inspected, while another mentions an official from Edfu, linked in some way with the nomadic Nubian group known as the Medjay, who appears to control a district close to the Kubban fortress. Dating to the late 12th and early 13th dynasties, the letters demonstrate the way in which the fortresses were controlled in the late Middle Kingdom, including rotations of personnel from Upper Egypt.

The fortresses as centres for mining and quarrying

The purpose of the fortresses at Faras and Serra, only about 15–25 kilometres (10–15 miles) north of Buhen, is not clear, since they appear to be associated neither with crucial trading points nor with centres of population (although the inclusion of part of the river within the defences at Serra perhaps suggests a concern with regulation of river traffic). The Faras and Serra forts provide strong support for the argument that, in the last resort, some Middle Kingdom Nubian fortresses were primarily architectural propaganda. However, many of the fortresses in Lower Nubia seem to have been strongly connected with mineral exploitation. Thus, Aniba may have originally had some connections with the gneiss quarries and carnelian mines at Gebel el-Asr, about 80 kilometres (50 miles) to the southwest. Since Aniba was located amid an area of relatively dense Nubian population it may have been the only Middle Kingdom garrison specifically intended as a military check on the Lower Nubians themselves. The northernmost fort, Kubban, 100 kilometres (60 miles) south of Aswan, was perhaps founded as early as the Old Kingdom; it was probably intended to protect the Egyptian copper and gold mining expeditions in the Wadi Allaqi.

The Wadi el-Hudi region was the primary location for amethyst mining in Egypt from the 11th Dynasty until the end of the Middle Kingdom, during which time the use of amethysts in jewellery reached a peak of popularity. Wadi el-Hudi stretches for about 12 km from northwest to southeast, with a complex network of ridges and smaller wadis spreading out across the surrounding area to the west and the east. The traces of ancient mining and quarrying expeditions are scattered throughout this adjacent region of smaller valleys rather than on the floor of the main wadi itself. Site 9 at Wadi el-Hudi is a large rectangular stone-built fort, the architectural style of which suggests that it was constructed in the 12th Dynasty and that it may be contemporary with the string of major mud-brick fortresses discussed above. To the northeast of the fortress are two amethyst mines, while to the northwest there is a short, well-preserved section of ancient road leading to a hill-top mining settlement probably founded in the late 11th Dynasty and quite likely in use at the same site time as the Site 9 fortress.

Despite being considerably smaller than the major Lower Nubian forts such as Buhen and Mirgissa, the Wadi el-Hudi fortress approaches the dimensions of lesser examples such as Semna South, Kumma or Shalfak. Even these last possess fortifications which are much thicker and stronger than the perimeter walls of the Wadi el-Hudi fortress. Comparisons are complicated by the second major consideration – almost all of the fortresses between the First Cataract and the Semna gorge are constructed of mudbrick rather than drystone walls. Wherever mudbrick was practical, the Egyptians seem to have employed it, and there is no doubt that it was the 'first choice' of their military architects. The fortified town at Kor is the only Egyptian site in Nubia defended by substantial drystone fortifications comparable to those at Wadi el-Hudi. Fortifications II and III at Kor were constructed of roughly hewn sandstone blocks, which had neither been squared nor dressed, and were laid in horizontal courses. Their curved bastions would have made them similar in appearance to the perimeter wall at Wadi el-Hudi. However, the fortified settlement at Kor, with its unusually elongated plan and its serpentine mudbrick outer wall, appears to have few other similarities to site 9 at Wadi el-Hudi.

It has been argued recently that Nubians and Egyptians may have used different techniques to construct dry-stone walls. It appears that the fortress at Wadi el-Hudi, as well as newly discovered fortresses associated with the el-Hisnein gold mines and Dihmit copper mines, which are situated south of Wadi el-Hudi, about 40–50 kilometres southeast of Aswan, all exhibit a similar Nubian-style dry-stone walling technique.

It should also be remembered, when comparing the shape of the Wadi el-Hudi fort with those of the Second Cataract forts, that the

Part of the external dry-stone wall of the Wadi el-Hudi 12th-Dynasty amethyst miners' fortress, c.1985–1795 BC.

plan of many of the forts most comparable in size – Semna South or Shalfak – was greatly influenced by their physical situation: the simple basic rectangles at Buhen, Aniba and Kubban apparently represent the preferred shape on a flat site. There are certain similarities between the Wadi el-Hudi fortress and its mudbrick counterparts that stand out: a tendency for walls to be built in straight lengths; a preference for compact rectangular plans; the use of projecting rounded bastions to defend the wall-angles; the provision of loopholes (although it has been argued recently that these are actually windows); and the construction of complex defended entrances. In respect of the bastions it is interesting to note that those at Wadi el-Hudi are similar to the *outer* defences of the major Egyptian forts in Nubia. The rounded bastions in the outer walls of the Second Cataract forts are often interpreted as a means of providing a line of fire over the encircling ditch (a feature entirely lacking at Wadi el-Hudi). This may well be the case, but the evidence at Wadi el-Hudi suggests that the outer wall with curved bastions should instead be regarded as one of the fundamental elements of Egyptian military architecture, regardless of the presence of ditches. All Second Cataract forts have a *pomoerium* (outer corridor) between the fortified perimeter wall and the internal buildings. On a lesser scale this seems to be repeated in the corridor around Building A, the principal internal building within the fortress at Wadi el-Hudi.

From the early 12th Dynasty onwards, the area between the first and fourth Nile cataracts was controlled by fortresses and watchtowers, some functioning almost as fortified depots rather than garrisons. This suggests an increasing concern with military control over the local Nubian population, utterly changing the political and economic contexts of trading and mining expeditions into the Middle Nile and surrounding deserts. The 12th-Dynasty amethyst mining settlements at Wadi el-Hudi appear to have been affected by this new military style of organization and bureaucracy that characterizes most Egyptian activities during the period. Miners were housed like colonists in a quasi-permanent settlement and amethysts were therefore procured and transported in a much more militarized and overtly controlled context, but also the effects of culture contact meant that even the architecture of the Site 9 fortress included apparent evidence of direct Nubian involvement, alongside Egyptians.

Tell Ras Budran, situated in the el-Markha plain, part of the southern Sinai coastal region, appears to have been the principal arrival point for expeditions to this major copper and turquoise mining region, via the Red Sea. In 2002–4, Gregory Mumford excavated a late Old Kingdom, fortified circular stone structure that had initially been recorded by Beno Rothenberg in 1967–68. The presence of this fortress suggests that South Sinai mining expeditions were considered to be in need of protection from attack. The circular design of the Tell Ras Budran fortress is unusual for an ancient Egyptian structure, and, like Site 9 at Wadi el-Hudi, it is also unusual in being a dry-stone construction rather than mud-brick.

The ultimate destination of many of the expeditions housed at Tell Ras Budran would have been the mines at Wadi Maghara, in the central southern Sinai, which were particularly exploited during the Old Kingdom and the early Middle Kingdom.

The Nubian frontier in the New Kingdom

In the New Kingdom, the original Middle Kingdom fortifications in Nubia were repaired and sometimes even elaborated (partly in response to such technological innovations as chariotry), but the settlements themselves became more like towns than garrisons; magnificent stone temples began to be built both inside and outside the bounds of the towers and bastions. New towns were established at such sites as Sesebi, Amara West, Kawa and Dokki Gel. Although these New Kingdom settlements were located further south than the Second

Cataract forts, their defences were perfunctory. The Egyptians of the New Kingdom obviously felt sufficiently confident of their control of Nubia to transfer their resources from fortifications to temples.

Amara West, situated on an island about 180 km south of Wadi Halfa, occupied an area of about 60,000 square metres, and was perhaps initially set up (probably in the reign of Seti I) as a base for gold-mining and trading expeditions further to the south. It had a political role in that it appears to have eventually taken over from the town of Soleb as the seat of the Deputy (*idnw*) of Kush (Upper Nubia). Originally excavated in the late 1930s, it has been excavated since 2008 by a team directed by Neal Spencer on behalf of the British Museum, whose new discoveries have included a previously unknown western suburb, incorporating a series of large villas.

The most completely excavated New Kingdom town in Nubia is Sesebi, situated in the Upper Nubian Abri-Delgo reach, between the 2nd and 3rd cataracts. It covered an area of more than 50,000 square metres, and the number of houses is thought to have been anything from 130 to 300, only a selection of which have survived and been excavated – the population has therefore been estimated at about 1,000–1,500. There were four gates through the enclosure wall, one in each side, and each gateway paved with stone, perhaps to facilitate wheeled vehicles entering Sesebi. Excavation findings suggest that the population of Sesebi was a specialized, state-run community rather than simply a cross-section of Egyptian society transplanted into Upper Nubia.

About a kilometre to the north of Kerma (the capital city of the Nubian culture of the same name) is the site of Dokki Gel ('red hill'), a significant New Kingdom settlement, which was briefly worked at by Reisner in about 1915, but only properly excavated from 1999, by Charles Bonnet. The defensive system of walls and ditches is identical to that of other Egyptian fortified towns north of the 3rd cataract. The southernmost of these major Egyptian towns was Kawa, known by the ancient name of Gem-Aten, located opposite Dongola in the heartland of the kingdom of Kerma.

The site of Kurgus, in the 5th-cataract region of Nubia, seems to represent the southern border of the New Kingdom empire in Nubia. It was here, on an outcrop known as the Hagar el-Merwa, that Thutmose I (*c.*1504–1492 BC) and Thutmose III (*c.*1479–1425

BC) both carved 'boundary stelae' marking their southern frontier. The choice of this spot for the stelae, close to the southern end of the so-called Korosko Road, suggests that an important overland trade-route, passing through the gold-bearing region of the Wadis Allaqi and Gabgaba, was probably already being used in the early New Kingdom.

The 'Ways of Horus'

Two Middle Kingdom literary texts *(The Tale of Sinuhe and The Prophecy of Neferti)* mention a fortress – or perhaps a whole sequence of fortifications – in the eastern Delta, known as the Walls of the Prince (*inbw ḥḳꜣ*), and apparently created around the time of the early 12th-Dynasty ruler Amenemhat I. In both texts, it is made clear that the purpose of the 'Walls' was to prevent 'Aamu' and 'Setjetyu' (ethnic groups usually interpreted as Asiatics) from entering Egypt. No Middle Kingdom archaeological remains directly identifiable with the Walls of the Prince have yet been found (although both Tell el-Retaba and Tell Hebua have been proposed). However, Eliezer Oren discovered five large Middle Kingdom settlements in northwest Sinai, and more than a hundred Middle Bronze Age II campsites across North Sinai as a whole. At Tel Ridan, Oren's excavations in the early 1970s revealed Middle Bronze Age II housing, a pottery kiln and a cemetery, including Egyptian pottery and scarabs.

By the New Kingdom there appears to have been a string of Egyptian fortresses in the eastern Delta and North Sinai that were sometimes described as the 'Ways of Horus' (*Wawat-Ḥr*). These are portrayed in some detail among a set of relief sculptures created on the external face of the northern wall of the hypostyle hall at Karnak temple during the reign of Seti I (see Chapter 3). The reliefs show the king's campaigns and battles in Western Asia and Libya, and they include a depiction of the king arriving back from a campaign against the Shasu bedouin, and entering the main fortress on Egypt's northeastern border. Known as Tjaru, the fortress was initially thought to have been located at the site of Tell Abu Sefa, where a Ramesside structure was excavated in 1840, but the archaeological remains of Tjaru are now thought to be located at Tell Hebua (in northwestern Sinai, about 9 km north of Tell Abu Sefa), which has been excavated by Mohammed Abd el-Maksoud from 1981 to the present. At Tell Hebua, a succession of Egyptian fortresses have been revealed, from the Second Intermediate Period fort through to the Ramesside period, the later phase covering a very large area (*c.*140,000 m^2) and including an inscribed block mentioning Tjaru. To the southeast of Tell Hebua is the site of Tell Borg, excavated by James Hoffmeier between 1999 and 2007, and incorporating the remains of a settlement, temple, cemetery and two phases of forts (with mud-brick and stone-lined moats) dating to the New Kingdom.

The fortresses at Hebua and Borg were clearly the starting point for the Ways of Horus, but Seti I's Karnak reliefs also show images of Egyptian fortresses further to the east. Excavations since the 1970s have gradually revealed a sequence of campsites and fortresses that map out the characteristic route taken by New Kingdom Egyptian armies heading overland from the Delta, along the northern edge of Sinai and into the Levant. Ten major clusters of these New Kingdom sites were discovered and excavated by Oren across northern Sinai, each including a fortified administrative complex, usually incorporating a well of some kind and surrounded by campsites that appear to have been occupied not only by Egyptian soldiers but also by other ethnic groups. These fortified settlements along the north Sinai seem to have been described as *khenemut* ('basins') by contemporary texts, thus probably stressing their primary role as watering places. One of them, Bir el-'Abd, comprised thirty campsites and a 1,600 m^2 fortress, including granaries and a water reservoir. Oren's excavations revealed Egyptian scarabs and pottery at Bir el-'Abd, as well as quantities of Levantine and Aegean ceramics. In the northeastern Sinai, he also uncovered the site of Haruba, which comprised twenty campsites centring on a set of 18th-Dynasty buildings (including a pottery workshop), which later developed into a 2,500 m^2 fortress from the reign of Seti I (*c.*1294–1279 BC) onwards.

Further archaeological work revealed another New Kingdom site near the eastern terminus of the Ways of Horus, in southern Palestine. Trude Dothan's 1972–82 excavations at Deir el-Balah, located in what is now the central Gaza strip, revealed a similar late 18th-Dynasty complex (including an elite residence), a possible artificial water reservoir, and a 400 m^2 Ramesside fortress. The burials in a cemetery associated with the fortress, the looting of which had alerted Dothan to the site, included a limestone anthropoid coffin, 50–60 Egyptian clay anthropoid coffins, as well as inscribed stelae.

The Libyan frontier in the New Kingdom

Prior to the late 18th Dynasty, the Western Desert appears to have been of little commercial or strategic interest to the Egyptian state. There also seems to have been no real indication that any significant military threat to Egypt was emanating from this area, compared with either Nubia or Western Asia. Before the New Kingdom, there is only minor evidence of trade (mainly focusing on ostrich eggs and feathers) and low-level raiding by long-known Libyan groups, identified by the Egyptian terms *tjemeh* and *tjehenu*. There are therefore few signs of any perceived need for fortifications or manpower either to protect this western border or to attempt any kind of colonization.

By *c.*1300 BC, however, this situation seems to have changed, and there are archaeological remains indicating increasing levels of Egyptian activity along the Mediterranean coastal strip to the west of modern Alexandria, including the creation of a Ramesside fortress-town at the site of of Zawiyet Umm el-Rakham (ZUR). This fortress seems to have lain at the western end of a chain of fortified settlements stretching from Tell Abqa'in in the western Delta, all of which were probably established by Ramesses II.

The ZUR fortress, covering an area of nearly 20,000 square metres, was first examined by Alan Rowe in 1948, and by Labib Habachi in the mid-1950s, but has been investigated by Steven Snape since 1994, revealing a much larger and more diverse set of structures than initially assumed. Finds include large quantities of imported pottery and other materials, suggesting that the site played a significant role in trade routes through the eastern Mediterranean. The role of the fortress therefore seems to have been closely connected with movement along the Mediterranean coastal strip by three significant groups: migrating Libyan groups (such as the Meshwesh and Libu, whose incursions it was presumably intended to deter), maritime traders, and the Egyptian army. A hieroglyphic inscription found in the main gate at ZUR refers to '*menenu*-fortresses upon the hill country of the Tjemehu and the wells within them'. Two wells have in fact been excavated at ZUR, and it has been argued that even just one of these would have been eminently capable of supplying the daily water needs (*c.*10,000 litres) of an estimated population of around 500 soldiers.

The fortress was probably founded early in the reign of Ramesses II, but it is also clear that it was probably abandoned during (or shortly after) his reign, given that no royal names apart from his have yet been found at the site. This evacuation and abandonment of the garrison was probably caused by the very factor for which it had been founded, i.e. the presence of 'Libyan' groups exerting eastwards pressure along the Marmarican coast towards Egypt. This pressure no doubt led eventually to Merenptah's war with the Meshwesh and Libu, documented in his fifth regnal year (c.1208 BC). According to Snape's excavations there is no significant occupation by Egyptian forces after Ramesses II and Merenptah, only ephemeral 'squatter' occupation, probably by local 'Libyan' indigenous peoples.

Egyptian fortifications in the Late Period

In the difficult times of the Third Intermediate Period and Late Period there was a renewed proliferation of fortifications both in Nubia and along Egypt's northeastern frontier with Western Asia. The stele of the 25th-Dynasty Kushite king Piankhi at Gebel Barkal, describing his victory over the Egyptians in 734 BC, mentions nineteen fortified settlements in Middle Egypt as well as 'walled cities' in the Delta region. Piankhi's own invasion of Egypt involved laying siege both to Hermopolis Magna and Memphis, as the Egyptian armies were driven further northward. Massive forts and walls continued to be built in Egypt – from Ramesses II's string of forts along the Mediterranean coast of the Delta to the Roman forts at Qasr Ibrim and Qasr Qarun (Dionysias) – but the sheer ambition and technical precocity of the Second Cataract fortifications remained unparalleled.

At the site of Dorginarti (on an island to the south of Buhen, in the northern part of the 2nd Cataract region), a group of mud-brick structures, enclosed within a fortified triangular enclosure wall, was originally assumed to be purely New Kingdom in date when excavated in 1964, but a reanalysis of the site by Lisa Heidorn in the early 1990s revealed that the earliest pottery at the site dated to the 8th–7th centuries BC (i.e. from the Third Intermediate Period to the Saite period). This site seems to have been abandoned by the late 6th century BC (the early part of the first Persian period), perhaps because of the inauguration of different military and trading routes through the eastern and western deserts or the Red Sea that may have bypassed Dorginarti.

It was during the Late Period that Egypt's northeastern frontier was penetrated several times by the Assyrians and Persians, and then finally by Alexander the Great. By the 1st millennium BC, there appears to have been a significant decline in Egyptian sites along the former Ways of Horus in northern Sinai, presumably as a result of the Assyrian conquest of the Levant and eventually also Egypt.

In 674 BC Taharqa (c.690–664 BC) was able temporarily to deter the invading forces of the Assyrian king Esarhaddon (c.680–669 BC), but in the ensuing decade the Assyrians made repeated successful incursions into the heart of Egypt, and it was perhaps only the periodic rebellion of Medes and Scythians at the other end of the Assyrian empire that prevented Esarhaddon from gaining a more permanent grip over the Egyptians. In 671 BC Esarhaddon captured Memphis, describing the event in an inscription at Senjirli:

> I laid siege to Memphis, Taharqa's royal residence, and conquered it in half a day by means of mines, breaches and assault ladders; I destroyed it, tore down its walls and burnt it down. His queen, the women of his palace, Ushanahuru, his heir apparent, his other children, his possessions, horses, large and small cattle beyond counting, I carried away as booty to Assyria. All Ethiopians I deported from Egypt – leaving not even one to do homage to me. Everywhere in Egypt, I appointed new local kings, governors, officers (*saknu*), harbour overseers, officials and administration personnel.

Three years later Taharqa had succeeded in briefly reasserting the Kushite hegemony over Egypt, while the Assyrians were distracted by problems elsewhere. By 667 BC, however, Esarhaddon's successor Ashurbanipal (c.668–627 BC) had penetrated beyond the Delta into Upper Egypt, where he must have severely damaged morale by pillaging Thebes, the spiritual home of the Egyptians. A fascinating insight into the campaigns of Esarhaddon and Ashurbanipal in Egypt has been provided by the survival of a fragment of relief from Ashurbanipal's palace at Nineveh (now in the British Museum) which shows the Assyrian army laying siege to an Egyptian city. The details of this scene, such as the depiction of an Assyrian soldier undermining the city-walls and others climbing ladders to the battlements, bear strong similarities with Egyptian siege representations described above, showing that ancient siege warfare from north Africa to Mesopotamia involved similar tactics and weaponry.

Eliezer Oren's excavations at the site of Tell er-Ruqeish (like the earlier site of Deir el-Balah, in the modern Gaza Strip), in 1982–84, revealed a 100,000 m² fortified settlement dating to the late 8th to 6th centuries BC. Ruqeish has been identified by Oren as Sargon II's so-called 'sealed harbour (*karum*) of Egypt', which is mentioned in the text inscribed on the Nimrud Prism ('I opened the sealed *karum* of Egypt. I mingled the Assyrians and Egyptians together; I made them trade with each other'). Ruqeish therefore seems to have functioned as a military headquarters and entrepot at the southwestern border of the Assyrian empire. The loss of the fortification surrounding the 6th-century BC phase of the town at Ruqeish has been interpreted as the dismantling or abandonment of this Assyrian control centre during a brief resumption of Egyptian imperialism in Syria-Palestine during the 26th Dynasty.

According to Herodotus, the 26th-Dynasty ruler Psamtek I (initially a vassal ruler for the Assyrians) established a garrison manned by Ionian and Carian mercenaries at Daphnae (Tell Defenna), in the eastern Delta. Petrie's 1886 excavations at Defenna both broadly confirmed Herodotus and provided new data, revealing a 375 × 630 m fortified settlement dating mostly to the time of Ahmose II, including iron smelting works, an impressive tower, and extensive storage buildings (see Chapter 7 for more detailed discussion of the identification of Daphnae as a naval base). Generally speaking, 26th-Dynasty fortifications concentrated at the western side of North Sinai. In 1974–76, Oren excavated a 40,000 square metre fort at Tell Qedwa (northwest Sinai), and a very similar Saite fortified settlement has been identified at Tell el-Maskhuta; it seems likely that both were frontier fortresses protecting the eastern Delta against Babylonian and Persian invasion. Like Defenna, these forts contained Egyptian, Phoenician and Greek pottery, weaponry and other artefacts. This archaeological data ties in with 26th-Dynasty textual references to Egyptian links with both Phoenician and Greek merchants and mercenary soldiers at this date. The late 7th- and early 6th-century BC destruction levels at Qedwa, Maskhuta and Defenna fortresses seem to corroborate textual references to Babylonian invasions in 601 and 568 BC, and later archaeological signs of severe disturbance also seem to tie in with the capture of these fortresses by the Persians in 525 BC.

In the First Persian Period there were at least two hundred Egyptian sites in northern Sinai, including a number of fortresses (as well as towns, villages, shrines, cemeteries and campsites). The excavations of a small fortress at Qatif yielded not only Egyptian pottery, but also many imported vessels, particularly of Greek and Phoenician origin, suggesting a strong commercial role played by the fort.

The significance of the Egyptian fortress

The motif of the doomed fortress, with its besieged residents looking out over their crenellated battlements, was one of the most enduring images of Egyptian warfare. The first depictions – on Protodynastic palettes and in the tomb scenes of the late Old Kingdom – tend to show the fortress in plan-form, as if viewed from above, but from the First Intermediate Period onwards side views appeared. These side views, in which the inhabitants are shown either defending frantically or making pleas for mercy and elaborate gestures of surrender, are one of the principal aspects of continuity between the early Middle Kingdom portrayals of battle and the New Kingdom depictions of Ramesside campaigns in Syria-Palestine.

To some extent, all Egyptian ceremonial buildings, including temples and funerary complexes, were intended to function as bastions of order and harmony (encapsulated by the Egyptian word *maat*), requiring at least symbolic fortifications to protect them from the surrounding chaos (*isfet*). Conversely, the distinctive features of Egyptian forts, with their symmetrical and often elegant designs, sometimes seem to reflect the monumental traditions of Egyptian religious architecture just as much as pragmatic military requirements.

CHAPTER 3

IMAGES AND NARRATIVES OF BATTLE IN THE NEW KINGDOM

The temple reliefs of the New Kingdom for the first time present quite detailed and panoramic scenes of Egyptian military campaigns. However, just as the iconography of battle on Protodynastic votive objects was already an idealization of the real situation, so it is likely that this process of simplification was carried over into the more elaborate arena of the pharaonic temple inscriptions and reliefs purporting to describe real military events, such as the battles at Megiddo and Qadesh, the evidence for which is described below.

These temple reliefs seem to have been often intended to illustrate basic universal concepts, such as the power of the king and the destruction or absorption of foreigners, they can rarely be relied upon to give anything more than incidental indications of the motivation and nature of Egyptian warfare. Indeed, the Egyptian archaeologist Gaballa Ali Gaballa has argued that the various 'panoramic vistas' of the battle of Qadesh on the temples of Ramesses II were effectively substitutes for the traditional smiting scene. The decision to depict the full details of battle was motivated primarily by artistic preference rather than by the desire to replace pure icons with real history.

During the early New Kingdom, most surviving temple walls are decorated with scenes of ritual and ceremony, primarily involving the king and a variety of deities. There are, however, also a few fragments of surviving 18th-Dynasty temple imagery that suggest the existence of a more dynamic and martial set of scenes portrayed on temple walls. Excavations in the 1990s revealed a few fragments of painted reliefs from the temple of the early 18th-Dynasty ruler Ahmose at Abydos that show parts of scenes of royal battle including chariots, archers and boats. Later in the dynasty there are relief blocks from the reigns of Amenhotep II and Tutankhamun that appear to show similar scenes of warfare involving chariotry. Towards the end of the 18th Dynasty there began to be some move towards depictions of narrative scenes that appeared to be set more specifically in a particular place and time. In the reign of Akhenaten, although ritual still dominated in the main temples, some scenes in the tombs of high officials at Amarna show a comparatively new kind of narrative art emerging. These funerary scenes show Akhenaten, Nefertiti and their subjects processing through the capital city in chariots or handing out rewards to loyal officials, providing a new sense of real people interacting with one another in recognizable cityscapes and natural landscapes. This growth in art that at least appears to be concerned with the representation of real, detailed, dynamic events eventually began to have a significant impact on the depiction of warfare.

In the reign of Seti I, although his mortuary temple at Abydos maintained the predominance of stiff scenes relating to temple ritual, a new kind of battle-oriented art appeared on the external northern side of the hypostyle hall at Karnak temple. Seti I's battle reliefs are already pre-figured in late 18th Dynasty in the form of small battle scenes, focusing on the king in his chariot, such as the images on the chariot of Thutmose IV and on the painted box of Tutankhamun. It is therefore possible that, if more of the decoration of 18th-Dynasty temples had survived (as evidenced by the fragments from Ahmose, Amenhotep II and Tutankhamun), we might well see that major, complex depictions of royal battles had already begun several generations before Seti I.

Nevertheless, Seti I's painted reliefs at Karnak are the earliest surviving intricate panoramas of specific Egyptian military campaigns and their aftermath. His Karnak reliefs document campaigns against the people and cities in Western Asia and also in the area now occupied by Libya. The reliefs can be divided into three registers on the left, and three on the right, with a doorway occupying the centre of the wall. Each register may represent an individual campaign, probably starting with the only one of the six that contains a date – the expedition in the first year of his reign, in which he crossed the Sinai peninsula and fought against the semi-nomadic Shasu, with the campaign probably culminating in a battle near the city of Gaza. The other two registers on the

Seti I in his chariot, fighting against Libyans, portrayed on the northern external wall of the Hypostyle Hall in the Temple of Amun at Karnak, c.1294–1279 BC.

left-hand-side show campaigns taking the Egyptians further north in Syria-Palestine, fighting against the city of Yenoam and then against further cities in the area of modern Lebanon. The scenes on the right show battles against the Hittites, now Egypt's main rivals for hegemony over Syria-Palestine, and also a campaign against the so-called Tjehenu (Libyans). All of the scenes are dominated by colossal images of the king in his chariot, at a massively larger scale than any other humans involved in the battles. An ostracon from the reign of Ramesses IV (Cairo, Egyptian Museum, CG 25124) bears a depiction of the king simultaneously charging in his chariot and ritually smiting the foe, surely indicating that these two standard icons of royal warfare in the New Kingdom were regarded as roughly equivalent and therefore largely interchangeable.

It is important to try to understand the relationship between Egyptian depictions of battle in the pharaonic period, and the actual battles themselves. How realistic were the images? Did the artists actually go to war? How representative and reliable are the surviving depictions of warfare at various dates? Were sketches made in the field of war and then later used as the basis for full-scale battle scenes, just as scribal diaries were used as the basis for full-blown literary accounts?

This last question is partly answered by scholars who have pointed out how closely the texts and reliefs portraying the battle of Qadesh interrelate. Of course this is not really an actual answer

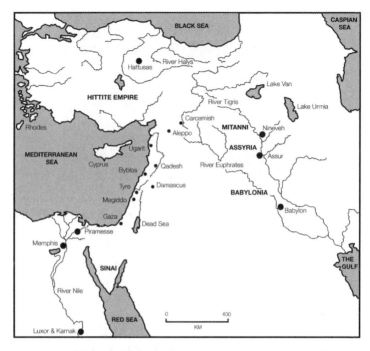

Map of Egypt and Western Asia in the Late Bronze Age. (Paul Vyse)

to the question because we know that the scribal campaign diary, although remaining at the core of many New Kingdom texts, was nevertheless largely transformed into a particular formal type of text divided up into conventional rhetorical sections. That the pictures closely mirror the words may simply indicate the extent to which the artistic form of the reliefs was dictated by the style and content of the texts. In other words the relationship between war art and war literature might not relate to the way in which they were each originally 'researched' but simply to a common set of conventions by which they were stylized to fulfil a joint religious purpose.

The battle of Megiddo (c. 1457 BC)

Egypt's main rival in the first half of the 18th Dynasty was Mitanni, a Hurrian kingdom sandwiched between the growing powers of

Hatti (i.e. the Hittites) and Assyria. By the time of Thutmose III, textual and visual sources indicate that Mitanni had established itself as the dominant influence on the city-states of northern Syria-Palestine. For the reign of Thutmose III's step-mother Hatshepsut there is currently no evidence of military campaigns in Western Asia, suggesting that perhaps the conquests of his grandfather, Thutmose I (who had placed a boundary stele as far north as the bank of the Euphrates) were being rapidly whittled away, primarily by the expansion of the Mitannian kingdom and its system of alliances with cities in the northern Levant. Judging largely from the so-called *Annals of Thutmose III* inscribed on the walls of part of the Temple of Amun at Karnak (and evidently based on the diary of the military scribe Tjeneni), this king seems to have lost no time in attempting to regain Egyptian hegemony over Syria-Palestine, evidently launching at least seventeen military campaigns into the region.

In the mid-15th century BC, during his first year on the throne as sole ruler, Thutmose III embarked on his initial expedition into the Levant, apparently to thwart a 'rebellion' of city-states led by the prince of Qadesh and doubtless backed by Mitanni. According to the *Annals*, he marched his army from the eastern Nile Delta, via Gaza and Yemma, to the plain of Esdraelon, leaving his general Djehuty to lay siege to the town of Joppa (modern Jaffa). According to a narrative preserved on the Ramesside Papyrus Harris 500 (now in the British Museum), Djehuty's men were smuggled into Joppa inside baskets. Whatever the truth of this story, Djehuty himself was a historical character and his tomb at Thebes contains an inscription describing his role in the campaign.

When Thutmose III arrived at Yemma he was informed that the enemy were waiting for him on the far side of the Carmel ridge, using the city of Megiddo (the Biblical Armageddon) as their base. The location of Megiddo was of great strategic influence in that it effectively controlled the Via Maris, which was the continuation of the 'Ways of Horus' route northwards, along the Levantine coast and up to Anatolia.

According to the *Annals*, a council of war took place between the king and his generals at Yemma – this is probably more of a literary device than a record of a real event, providing the narrator of the *Annals* with an opportunity to demonstrate the king's bravery and tactical abilities. There appear to have been three possible strategies:

to follow the most direct route across the ridge, emerging about a mile from Megiddo; to take the path northwards to the town of Djefty, emerging to the west of Megiddo; or to take the more southerly route via the town of Taanach, about five miles southeast of Megiddo. Against the generals' advice, Thutmose is said to have chosen the most dangerous approach – the direct route – which would take the army through a narrow pass, forcing them to march slowly one after the other, relying solely on the element of surprise.

The journey across the Carmel range took three days, ending with a lengthy but safe passage through the narrow defile. The army then descended onto the plain and immediately found themselves within a few hundred yards of the confederation of Asiatic troops, encamped for the night in front of the city of Megiddo. The following morning Thutmose III's troops launched a frontal attack that routed the enemy, described (with some hyperbole presumably) as 'millions of men, hundreds of the thousands of the greatest of all lands, standing in their chariots'. In their haste to take shelter in Megiddo, the fleeing troops were said to have accidentally locked out the kings of Qadesh and Megiddo, who had to be dragged up onto the battlements by their clothing. After a seven-month siege the city was captured, bringing the campaign to a successful conclusion.

It is important to bear in mind, however, that the *Annals*, as a particular genre of official inscription, cannot be taken in any sense at face value as a purely factual, historical document – in particular, the theme of the king contradicting his generals is one that is encountered elsewhere as a kind of royal trope that may have been effectively a piece of fiction intended to show that Thutmose III was acting in the 'correct' kingly way. It seems likely, on the other hand, on the basis of roughly contemporaneous archaeological and textual data, that the general basis of the foreign policy presented in the *Annals* is reflective of real places and events relating to the Egyptian presence in Syria-Palestine at this time.

Thutmose III backed up his military achievements in Syria-Palestine with the creation of a network of garrisons and numerous vassal treaties. In his sixth campaign he adopted a more long-term strategy, taking back 36 chiefs' sons to the Egyptian court so that they could be held as hostages, indoctrinated with Egyptian ideas and eventually restored to their thrones as puppet-rulers. Egyptian officials, such as the general Djehuty, began to be appointed as viceroys in Retenu (the geographical term used at this date to refer to the southern Levant), bearing the Akkadian titles *rabisu* (commissioner/governor) and *sakinu* (resident) and probably having equal rank with the local princes.

By the 14th century BC there seem to have been three such Egyptian *rabisu*s in Syria-Palestine, corresponding to the administrative zones of Amurru, Upi and Canaan. The three *rabisu*s formed a court of arbitration to settle disputes between the vassal princes, and there was regular correspondence, via royal envoys, between the princes, *rabisu*s and the pharaoh. Occasionally the local princes complained about the conduct of a *rabisu*, as in the letter from Ribaddi, the ruler of Byblos, protesting that Pakhura, the *rabisu* of Upi, had overstepped the mark in allocating a troop of bedouin soldiers to the city militia.

The battle of Qadesh

Ramesses II was perhaps the last pharaoh with realistic imperial ambitions in Syria-Palestine. Like Thutmose III, he had grown up in an age when, according to many researchers, the northern provinces of Retenu were neglected and allowed to slip gradually out of Egyptian control. This time, however, the empire that was benefiting from Egypt's weakness was not Mitanni (now in irreversible decline) but the increasingly powerful Hittites. During the years of the Amarna period and its aftermath, it seems likely that the Hittites took advantage of the power vacuum in Retenu while Egypt was absorbed in its own internal struggles. According to a cuneiform tablet from the archives of the Hittite capital of Hattusas (modern Boghazköy), Suppiluliumas I – the Hittite king who had defeated King Tushratta of Mitanni and effectively usurped the pharaohs' role as dominant power in the Levant – even received a plea from a widowed late 18th-Dynasty queen (perhaps Ankhsenamun, the wife of Tutankhamun) to allow her to marry a Hittite prince.

Despite an apparently resounding victory over the Hittites at Qadesh (*c.*1290 BC), Ramesses II's father Seti I had come to an agreement with the Hittite king Muwatallis by which Qadesh and

Amurru (the northernmost province of Retenu) were retained by the Hittites, in return for the guarantee that they would not interfere with Egyptian interests in Canaan and Upi. This must have seemed a satisfactory solution at the time, but for Ramesses II – casting himself very much in the role of Thutmose III – it is possible that only total control of Syria-Palestine would suffice.

In the summer of the fourth year of his reign (*c*.1275 BC), Ramesses succeeded in consolidating Egyptian control of the provinces of Canaan and Upi and recaptured Amurru without coming into direct conflict with the Hittites. He then forced Benteshina, the prince of Amurru, to sign a vassal treaty with Egypt. Since, however, the Hittites by now regarded Amurru as a legitimate part of their empire, the Hittite texts indicate that Muwatallis swore a sacred oath that he would regain the Syrian territories and crush the Egyptian king. For his part, Ramesses was now keen to capitalize on his successes by pushing forward into the area of central Syria and the city of Qadesh. The location of Qadesh is now recognised as the archaeological site of Tell Nebi Mend, a tell on the Homs plain in present-day Syria, excavated by a team from University College London, under the directorship of Peter Parr between the 1970s and the early 1990s.

The scene was set, in the spring of 1274 BC, for the battle of Qadesh, a Bronze Age conflict that is even better documented than that at Megiddo. There are at least thirteen surviving Egyptian versions of the battle, in three different forms (a Poem, Bulletin and Reliefs) recorded both on papyri and on the walls of Ramesses' temples in Egypt and Nubia. The plan adopted by Ramesses in his second campaign was to send a particular section of his army (described as the '*na'arn*') northwards via the Phoenician coast, while the main army, divided into four divisions (named Amun, Pre, Ptah and Seth), marched through Canaan and Upi, eventually approaching Qadesh from the south. Meanwhile, Muwatallis had assembled an army which, according to Egyptian estimates, consisted of 2,500 chariots and 37,000 infantrymen: more than double the size of the Egyptian forces. Ramesses' army appears to have marched untroubled through the newly pacified southern territories of Retenu. After a journey of about a month the main Egyptian army was passing through the 'wood of Labni', just a few miles to the south of Qadesh, and preparing to ford the River Orontes. At this point they captured two Shasu bedouin, who convinced them that the Hittites were still many miles to the north in the region of Aleppo. Ramesses therefore is said to have marched on ahead with the first division, Amun; he then began to set up camp near Qadesh, planning to lay siege to it the following day.

It soon emerged, through the capture of two Hittite spies, that Muwatallis and his army were already encamped nearby – just on the other side of Qadesh – and ready to attack. Unfortunately, however, the Pre division of the Egyptian army was still on its way from the River Orontes to the new camp, while the two other divisions were still in the Wood of Labni. Before anything could be done to remedy this situation the Hittite chariots launched their attack, taking the Pre division by surprise and sending them fleeing north towards the Egyptian camp. It was then that Ramesses is supposed to have valiantly rallied the combined troops of Amun and Pre in an attempt to rescue the situation. Although he is quoted as saying 'Hold your ground and steady yourself my shield bearer! I will attack them like the swoop of the falcon, killing, slaughtering and casting them to the ground', it is clear that the Egyptians and their king might have been totally overwhelmed at this stage if it had not been for the timely arrival of the *na'arn* troops who had come by the coastal route and marched eastwards to Qadesh. With the aid of the *na'arn*, the Amun and Pre divisions were able to regroup and push back the Hittite chariotry, thus affording valuable breathing space so that the Ptah and Seth divisions could catch up with the rest.

The next stage of the conflict took place the following morning, as the two armies faced each other on either side of the Orontes. The Hittites still had the numerical advantage but they had probably suffered heavy losses in their chariotry. Ramesses kept the initiative by launching an attack across the river – this was at first victorious but eventually, through sheer weight of numbers, a situation of stalemate set in. In the subsequent exchange of envoys an uneasy peace was made, allowing each party to claim some degree of success. Ramesses, however, refused to make a treaty as his father had done and he returned to Egypt with the control of Amurru still unresolved. Moreover, as soon as he had retreated the Hittites not only regained control of Amurru, sending prince Benteshina into exile, but also pushed down into Upi, thus once more reducing the Egyptian empire to the borders of the province of Canaan. Once again, as with Thutmose III's *Annals*, the visual and textual accounts of Ramesses II's campaigns in Syria-Palestine, which form the primary sources for the last few paragraphs discussing the battle of Qadesh, should be regarded as a particular genre of communication functioning very much as part of the elite control of the Egyptian state rather than as purely historical records – they need to be interpreted carefully rather than simply being treated naively as accurate accounts of real events.

Although Ramesses II clearly regarded the battle of Qadesh as the peak of his entire reign, there can be little doubt that it was actually the last flourish of the Egyptian empire. In about 1259 BC he was finally obliged to make a treaty with a new Hittite king, Hattusilis III. One major incentive to this treaty would have been that Egypt and the Hittites both by then faced a growing threat from the Assyrian empire of Shalmaneser I (*c*.1273–1244 BC). The treaty was recorded on silver tablets in cuneiform and hieroglyphs, copies of which have survived in the form of inscriptions in Karnak temple and the Ramesseum, as well as a clay tablet in the Boghazköy archives. The new links with the Hittites were celebrated by marriages between Ramesses and various Hittite princesses, just as Amenhotep III had cemented the alliance with Mitanni by marrying the princesses Tadukhipa and Gilukhipa. For the rest of the Ramesside Period the control of the Levant was probably a matter more for envoys than soldiers.

Tremendous publicity was given to the battle of Qadesh, as we have noted above. Although the scale of the commemoration implies that it was intended to be regarded as a high point in Ramesses II's reign, it seems likely that it was at best a case of stalemate, and at worst a severe setback to Ramesses' empire-building. These temple reliefs were essentially religious artefacts rather than historical documents. Since they were primarily dealing with basic universal concepts, such as the power of the king and the destruction of non-Egyptians, they cannot be relied upon to give anything more than incidental

The Egypto-Hittite peace treaty, inscribed on the western wall of the Cachette Court of the Temple of Amun at Karnak, c.1258 BC.

indications of the motivation and nature of warfare. It seems likely that the ideology they express continued to be useful in the context of religion and propaganda (and the location on the exterior walls of temples seems to make it clear that this was at least one of the aims of the battle reliefs), but that the real attitudes of the king and his generals and soldiers had actually moved on, so that they were fighting for pragmatic economic and political gain rather than simply fulfilling their duties to the gods.

The reliefs depicting the battle of Qadesh incorporate depictions of the interior of Ramesses's main encampment near the River Orontes. The camp was surrounded by a rectangular stockade, and the scenes include activities relating to the supply of food and maintenance of equipment. Among the details are ox-carts carrying supplies into the camp, a chariot in the course of being repaired, an archer re-stringing his bow, and a seated soldier whose leg-wound is in the process of being tended. Ramesses' magnificent tent is shown surrounded by the smaller tents of his officers, and there are also a number of dramatic tableaux including depictions of the seated king discussing strategy with his generals and the interrogation and beating of Hittite spies. The scene of chariot repairs in Ramesses II's Qadesh camp also emphasizes the ongoing process of maintenance of weaponry and equipment, whether in garrisons or in the encampments of a campaigning armies. In a letter dating to the reign of Ramesses II sent by Kenamun the scribe to Huy the charioteer, the writer points out 'My lord's horses are in very good shape, for I am giving them grain daily'.

In **Egyptian military camps,** apart from the individuals involved in producing food and weapons for the army, there were also many other workers making a wide range of non-military contributions to the cause. The Theban tomb of Userhet, an army officer in the time of Amenhotep II, contains scenes of barbers and quartermasters handing out the rations. A number of reliefs from the tomb of Horemheb at Saqqara (built and decorated during his career as a general, before he became king) depict a military encampment dating to the reign of Tutankhamun (c.1336–1327 BC). One recently excavated fragment shows a tent already pitched and another perhaps in the process of being erected, surrounded by soldiers preparing and eating food. Three better-preserved fragments from the same tomb (now in the Berlin and Bologna museums) show boys carrying water-skins and food around the camp while the soldiers tend horses and donkeys, maintain the chariotry equipment and set up tents. Views of the tents of the army officers (including perhaps that of Horemheb himself) show that they contain stocks of food and a folding stool and are being fastidiously cleaned and dusted inside by servants. In one of these scenes a squatting scribe is shown writing instructions or perhaps a list of provisions; the presence of such scribes and servants must have considerably added to the numbers of men in the professional armies of the pharaonic period. The unusually well-developed bureaucratic wing of the New Kingdom Egyptian military system probably transformed the army itself into the long arm of the Egyptian scribe, reaching out into foreign countries to obtain the materials, livestock and manpower that the maintenance of temple and state demanded.

Tomb paintings at Saqqara

As well as the Ramesside battle reliefs discussed above, there were also some non-royal tombs of the 18th–20th dynasties that contained images relating to military exploits. For the 18th Dynasty, the best-known are those in the tomb of Horemheb at Saqqara, which is one of the group of late New Kingdom elite burials to the south of the causeway of Unas. This tomb was created and decorated during

Scene in the tomb of Horemheb at Saqqara showing Nubian prisoners being guarded by Egyptian soldiers wielding batons, c.1330 BC.

Horemheb's long career prior to becoming king, when he served as a general under Tutankhamun and Aye. Among the many scenes in his tomb relating to military life and foreign relations is a depiction of life in a New Kingdom military camp (see box above), which has parallels with the portrayals of the camp occupied by Ramesses II's army incorporated in the temple reliefs representing the battle of Qadesh. Another scene shows several Nubian prisoners, depicted with curly hair and earrings, all seated on the ground submissively, as three Egyptian soldiers with batons watch over them. A scribe is shown, perhaps writing a report on the capture of the Nubians, and, according to the accompanying hieroglyphic text, two prisoners were being selected as servants for the royal court. Further scenes show a pair of chariots and their crew, as well as a group of grovelling foreign rulers being presented to Tutankhamun by Horemheb.

In 2017 a new 19th-Dynasty tomb was discovered at Saqqara, in a New Kingdom cemetery to the east of the group within which Horemheb's tomb was located. This funerary monument belonged to a man called Iwrhya, who served as a general in the time of Seti I and Ramesses II and probably had non-Egyptian origins. The military scenes in this tomb include one section that, as with Horemheb's tomb, appears to parallel part of a royal relief. Thus, one block portrays soldiers in chariots passing across a crocodile-filled canal, which closely resembles the canal represented in part of the Karnak reliefs of Seti I, described above, where the royal chariot is shown advancing through the area around the fortress of Tjaru, about to

Scene in the tomb of Horemheb at Saqqara showing two chariots and crew, c.1330 BC.

embark on a campaign against the Shasu bedouin in Western Asia. Iwrhya's tomb also includes a depiction of Syro-Palestinian boats from which a cargo of wine amphorae is being unloaded, indicating the benefits of Egyptian control over Syria-Palestine.

The last flourish of temple battle reliefs

The latest surviving major example of a New Kingdom panoramic battle relief is to be found at the mortuary temple of the 20th-Dynasty ruler Ramesses III in western Thebes (Medinet Habu). Here, the northern exterior wall is decorated with episodes from his victorious war against the Sea Peoples and Libyans. The military theme is also continued in the reliefs around the walls of the first court of Medinet Habu, in which it is made clear from the inscriptions that the booty from the king's campaigns (including the severed hands and foreskins of his enemies) was physically brought here to be piled up in the presence of the great god Amon-Ra. Some of the reliefs below the window show that the king would also have viewed wrestling matches here, involving Egyptians competing against Libyans, Nubians or Asiatics.

Unlike the others described above, the war against the Sea Peoples was clearly primarily defensive, taking place on Egyptian soil and coastal waters. Historically speaking, it is therefore not only the last real flourish of the temple battle relief but also the first that dwells on the struggle simply to maintain Egyptian control of its borders rather than inexorably expanding outwards. It is also of course the only known example of this kind of relief to portray a sea battle, and this must have provided an interesting problem for the artists: how to incorporate the king into a maritime scene in which chariot warfare would be totally out of place? The artists' solution was to show the chariot essentially 'parked' behind the king, while he himself stands with bow fully drawn and an arrow in place, facing into the naval action. He can therefore be shown to be taking an active part in the battle without the awkwardness of either attempting to balance him precariously (at his usual larger-than-life scale) in a boat, and without excluding the chivalrous paraphernalia of chariot warfare.

There are a surprising number of instances in which Ramesside artists portray royal action that is more complex and specific than simply the standard icon of the king firing arrows from his chariot. Thus, a scene in the forecourt of the Luxor Temple shows Ramesses II in the act of stepping onto his chariot, and three other scenes in the same forecourt portray standing figures of the same ruler, two showing him standing in front of defeated fortresses (in the act of receiving the tribute of defeated leaders) and the third presenting him in hand-to-hand combat, apparently in the final stages of conquest of a fortified town.

The New Kingdom battle scenes, and accompanying inscriptions, represent a key element of the classic view that we have concerning the 'official' point of view of the Egyptian state, in which the individual details of military campaigns and skirmishes often appear to be subservient to cosmological and ideological visions of Egypt and the pharaoh as defenders of truth and harmony in a dangerous world. The next chapter discusses the use of this kind of evidence in an attempt to understand the motivations and consequences of Egyptian warfare.

CHAPTER 4

WHY DID WARS HAPPEN AND HOW WERE THEY EXPERIENCED?

WHAT DO WE KNOW ABOUT THE ancient Egyptians' political and economic motivations for warfare? In the visual and written evidence, such issues as the defence of borders and the acquisition of valuable land, livestock, natural resources and slaves were all frequently masked, to some extent, by layers of religion and ritual, providing both moral justification and a 'universal' framework. Much of the evidence, even when it appears to relate to specific events, is actually communicating features of the official view of Egyptian battle. However, evidence concerning the real lived experience of the individual in Egyptian warfare is much more elusive and awkward. There are many crucial questions for which we have only partial answers. What was the role of each member of the army, whether elite charioteer or Nubian archer? How did individuals react to the rigours of battle and what were their rewards, if any?

This chapter also explores the intriguing evidence for the types of injuries inflicted on the battlefield, including anthropological evidence, as well as images and texts, such as skeletal remains from a wide variety of sites and dates, that can sometimes provide valuable data on the types of injuries inflicted on the battlefield; anthropological evidence of this type is a crucial means of verifying and complementing the details of the surviving textual and pictorial descriptions of Egyptian battle.

Official views of battle and its aims

Numerous aspects of the evidence for Egyptian warfare, from Protodynastic votive objects to New Kingdom royal battle reliefs, were part of the essential infrastructure of the temples, and therefore must have often reflected the religious and economic concerns of priests rather than soldiers. Since the first known hieroglyphic texts appear to have developed partly out of early Egyptian accounting systems, it is not surprising that later Egyptian writings sometimes retain a little of the flavour of the account book – in the case of texts and paintings evoking battles there was always the potential for an unusually economic slant. This is perhaps most vividly illustrated by a detail from the Abu Simbel reliefs of the battle of Qadesh, showing a scribe dutifully recording the number of severed hands taken from the enemy. The resulting blinkered view of battle as a kind of necessary preliminary to the totting up of spoils and dead is partly a product of the predominant literary form but, for similar reasons, it must also be an accurate insight into the official Egyptian view of battle, since the art and warfare of ancient Egypt were both equally dominated by the temple-based scribal elite.

The unusually well-developed bureaucratic wing of the New Kingdom Egyptian military system probably transformed the army itself into the long arm of the Egyptian scribe, reaching out into foreign countries to obtain the materials, livestock and manpower that the maintenance of temple and state demanded. This would suggest that the heroicism of the Qadesh battle reliefs was largely an affectation, sweetening the pill of the remorseless credit and debit of the scribal account book.

Although the social and political motivation behind Egyptian warfare and 'colonization' is still not properly understood, it seems likely that battle was regarded by the Egyptian state not as an opportunity for heroism or even territorial gain but as just another commercial expedient, comparable with trading or quarrying, whereby large quantities of certain commodities might be procured by force. Indeed the word often translated as 'army' or 'host' – *mšᶜ* – appears to be used relatively indiscriminately to refer to all types of expeditionary force, whether military or civil.

In a groundbreaking study of the relations between Egypt and the Levant, Donald Redford provided a succinct analysis of the emerging rationale for Egyptian warfare in Syria-Palestine during the Early Dynastic period: 'cheap manpower rapidly became what Egypt expected to receive from the adjacent lands, along with booty, enforced benevolences, gifts, and raw materials, as part of their obligations to Egypt ordained by the gods. Egypt sought to ensure a regular supply, not through the establishment of an imperial infrastructure permanently subjugating foreign lands, but through intimidation and the creation of a "sphere of influence" ' (Redford, *Egypt, Canaan and Israel...*, 1992: 51).

The Egyptians' principal motivations for attacking foreigners were probably also connected with such factors as the maintenance and extension of their own borders, the protection of trading and quarrying expeditions, and the acquisition of foreign goods, raw materials and extra manpower. It is evident from some of the texts, however, that their armies were often despatched for purposes which were, in the short term at least, essentially negative and destructive – they might be sent to punish and terrify the pharaoh's enemies, usually to maintain the 'sphere of influence'. Such acts are often described as motivated by the need to 'pacify' (*sḥtp*) the 'rebels'. It has been argued that these raids were an integral part of Egyptian diplomacy. Thus attacks on fortified towns may well have been shock tactics intended either to create favourable alliances or to acquire new vassal states or towns, after which, more diplomatic methods (e.g. marriages between royal princes' daughters and the Egyptian ruler) may have been used to maintain these international relationships.

The early New Kingdom *Stele of Kamose* is a classic instance of Egyptian antecedents for the Classical Greeks' ravaging of the agricultural resources of defeated enemies, but the history of the destruction of enemies' agricultural resources can actually be found much earlier in Egyptian history – the funerary biography of Weni, for instance, includes a poetic celebration of the destruction of the land and homes of the 'sand-dwellers' (a term assumed to refer to Asiatics): 'This army returned in safety, it had ravaged the sand-dwellers' land...it had flattened the sand-dwellers' land...it had sacked its strongholds...it had cut down its figs, its vines...it had thrown fire in all its [mansions]…it had slain its troops by many ten-thousands…[it had carried off] many [troops] as its captives'.

A similar approach appears to have been taken to Nubian 'rebels' in the Middle Kingdom, to judge from the stele of Intefiker, probably a high official of Amenemhat I, in which he states: 'Then I went upstream in victory, slaughtering the Nubian in his (own) land, and came back downstream stripping crops, and cutting down the rest of their trees, so that I could put fire to their homes, as is done against a rebel against the king'. Donald Redford even goes so far as to suggest that the Egyptian policy of destroying the agricultural land and fortresses of their Asiatic enemies may have contributed significantly to the decline in urbanism in post-Early Bronze Age III Palestine. There seems to have been an emerging official rationale for Egyptian warfare in Syria-Palestine from as early as the Early Dynastic period, when it perhaps first became apparent to the Egyptians that cheap manpower could be obtained from the Levant, along with looted items and materials. All of this warfare could be 'justified' on the grounds that they were part of foreign leaders' obligations to Egypt ordained by the gods. The surviving records indicate that this regular supply of prisoners and booty was achieved not by establishing a permanent imperial infrastructure but through periodic bouts of intimidation, which allowed them to effectively create something that might now be described as a blend of economic imperialism and gunboat diplomacy. This analysis could refer even to the much later periods, such as the New Kingdom, when Egypt is supposed to be a great imperial power, but might still be said to operate in Syria-Palestine as a kind of exploitative drain on the economy rather than a permanently maintained occupying, colonizing or imperial influence.

The soldiers' experience

The experience of the individual soldier is only rarely elucidated through texts, images or archaeology. What was the role of each member of the army; how did individuals react to the rigours of battle; and what were their rewards, if any? A reasonably clear distinction may be made between the pictorial and textual evidence: both are more concerned with the results and rewards of battles than with the battles themselves, but the pictorial evidence can at least be relied upon to provide certain details of soldiers going about their business. Virtually all texts describing warfare are largely made up of the listing of booty, either acquired by the king/state in general or by the individual.

Funerary narrations of military exploits are to be found on certain stelae as early as the Middle Kingdom, notably those of the general Nesumenthu (Louvre, C 1) and the military official Khusobek (Manchester Museum, 3306). John Baines summarizes the significance of the stele of Khusobek as follows, stressing the formulaic nature of the text: 'As in many texts recounting personal exploits, there is no neat conclusion. The structure of each episode is: context; action; reward. The reward documents the protagonist's status and his veracity' (Baines, *The Stele of Khusobek*, 1987: 55). Baines notes that, as in most texts of this type, Khusobek concentrates on the rewards

Stele of Khusobek, dating to the reign of Senusret III, h. 28cm, w. 16.5cm, c.1874–1855 BC (Manchester Museum). (Ian Shaw, after Eric Peet, The Stela of Sebek-khu, Manchester University Press, 1914: Pl.I)

he achieved through battle rather than the historical significance of the events. It is also suggested, somewhat tenuously perhaps, that the style of the text is sufficiently similar to the later 'royal annals' genre of the 18th Dynasty to imply that it was borrowing its style from that of still-undiscovered 'royal narrative inscriptions' from Middle Kingdom temples, which would perhaps have been antecedents of the 18th-Dynasty annals.

Ahmose son of Ibana, an admiral whose lifetime spanned the reigns of Ahmose, Amenhotep I and Thutmose I, describes the major events of his career on the walls of his tomb at Elkab. The expulsion of the hated Hyksos rulers – an Asiatic elite group who controlled northern Egypt during the Second

Intermediate Period (*c.*1650–1550 BC) – may have represented the restoration of Egyptian pride and native rule on an abstract political level, but Ahmose's summary of the campaign amounts to a personal shopping list ('Then Avaris was despoiled, and I brought spoil from there: one man, three women; total, four persons. His majesty gave them to me as slaves'), and the culmination of his career came in the form of the capture of 'a chariot, its horse and him who was on it as a living captive'. Obviously a 'funerary autobiography' of this type was designed to enumerate the virtues and possessions of the deceased, and the application of the modern term 'autobiography' is extremely misleading, decontextualizing a form of text inevitably geared more to the offering list than to the historical narrative. Ahmose's text is simply an extended version of the lists of actions and rewards recorded on private funerary stelae.

Papyrus Lansing: satirizing soldiers

The ideal antidote to such eulogies of the benefits of battle, however, is to be found in Papyrus Lansing: a 'schoolbook' for scribes designed to show the superiority of their own profession by giving a jaundiced account of all other trades (hence its usual title: *Be a Scribe*). The section describing the life of the Egyptian soldier lays gleeful emphasis on the hardships endured:

> Come let me tell you the woes of the soldier…He is called up for Syria. He may not rest. There are no clothes, no sandals. The weapons of war are assembled at the fortress of Sile. His march is uphill through mountains. He drinks water every third day; it is smelly and tastes of salt. His body is ravaged by illness. The enemy comes, surrounds him with missiles and life recedes from him. He is told, "Quick forward, valiant soldier! Win for yourself a good name!" He does not know what he is about. His body is weak, his legs fail him. When victory is won, the captives are handed over to his majesty to be taken to Egypt. The foreign woman faints on the march; she hangs herself (on) the soldier's neck. His knapsack drops, another grabs it while he is burdened with the woman…If he leaps and joins the deserters, all his people are imprisoned. He dies on the edge of the desert, and there is none to perpetuate his name. He suffers in death as in life….

This satirical account is deliberately intended to paint an exaggeratedly black picture of military life, but it does help to correct the impression given by such men as Ahmose son of Ibana that the life of the campaigning soldier was one long succession of enemy captives and severed enemy hands. With a clever insight into the travails of battle, the scribe even manages to imply not only that the acquisition of a female captive might turn out to be to the detriment of the soldier but that the all-important booty might revert to the king rather than the individual. It is also interesting to note the assertion that a deserter's family would be thrown into jail – even if overstated, it suggests that desertion may have been discouraged by threats of reprisals on a man's relations.

Apart from these relatively 'formal' descriptions of battle, whether positive or negative, there is an alternative body of evidence for the soldiers' view of battle, in the form of private and official letters relating to military life, such as the Semna Despatches, some of the Amarna Letters, and various items of correspondence to and from individual soldiers. The forms of these texts are arguably as 'literary' as the inscriptions on the walls of temples and tombs, but it is in terms of their content that they have a greater claim to objectivity. They are all essentially private communications, whereas the reliefs and paintings – even of private individuals – were intended to be placed on display as integral parts of the Egyptian religious and funerary systems.

The Semna Despatches

The Semna Despatches are a set of 12th-Dynasty papyri comprising copies of reports sent to the commander at Thebes from the Egyptian garrison at Semna West in Nubia. None of the despatches contain dates relating to any particular reign, but one of them refers to a man called Simonthu who is known from other texts to have lived in the time of Amenemhat III. The texts convey something of the tedium of military life in between campaigns or battles. Despatch 4 describes the routine task of desert surveillance: 'Another letter brought to him [a high-ranking officer at Semna West] from the liegeman Ameny who is at Khesef-Medjau ['Repeller of the Medjay': Serra East fortress], being a message sent by fortress to fortress…The patrol that went out to patrol the desert-edge near the fortress of Khesef-Medjau on the last day of the third month of spring in the third year has returned to report to me, saying "We have found the track of 32 men and 3 donkeys…" '.

Despatch 3 (sent from Iken fortress, identified with the site of Mirgissa) presents information that suggests that the Egyptians were closely monitoring the movements of the so-called Medjay, a nomadic Nubian ethnic group: 'It is a communication to your scribe (life, prosperity, health) about the fact that those two guardsmen and seventy Medjay-people who went following that track in month 4 of Peret, day 4, came to report to me on this day, at the time of evening, having brought three Medjay-men … saying "We found them on the desert edge, below the inscription of Shemu, likewise three women", so said they. Then I questioned these Medjay-people, saying "Where have you come from?". Then they said, "We have come from the well of Ibhet".'

There are also references to trade taking place in the vicinity of the fortresses – so Despatch 7, evidently sent from Semna West fortress to one of the others, reads: 'What they had brought was traded. They sailed upstream to the place whence they had come, bread and beer having been given to them…'.

Single combat in the Middle Kingdom

Detailed accounts of battle have survived best in what might be described as the purely literary record (a genre that evolved in Egypt partly in response to the need for exercises to be repeatedly copied by trainee scribes). One of the few surviving verbal descriptions of the individual experience of battle is the 12th-Dynasty literary narrative, *The Tale of Sinuhe*. It is interesting to note, however, that the fundamental aspects of this account of single-handed combat are very similar to the basic elements of large-scale battle, as portrayed in temple and tomb decoration:

> At night I strung my bow, sorted my arrows, practised with my dagger, polished my weapons…He came toward me while I waited, having placed myself near him…he raised his battle-axe and shield, while his armful of weapons fell toward me. When I had made his weapons attack me, I let his arrows pass by me without effect, one following the

other. Then, when he charged me, I shot him, my arrow sticking in his neck; he screamed; he fell on his nose; I slew him with his axe…Then I carried off his goods; I plundered his cattle. What he had meant to do to me I did to him. I took what was in his tent; I stripped his camp. Then I became great, wealthy in goods, rich in herds.

Sinuhe's antagonist is injured by bow and arrow from a distance and then killed with an axe at close quarters, thus paralleling, in microcosm, the battle tactics depicted in late Old Kingdom and Middle Kingdom tombs, whereby units of archers and squads of infantry armed with spears and axes were the two basic elements of the army. This raises the question as to whether real-life confrontations between individual combatants were miniature versions of the full-scale pitched battles or whether the writer of *The Tale* is deploying a standard battle narrative in an inappropriate context (particularly given that the account of post-duel plundering does not really fit with the one-to-one character of the struggle itself). Sinuhe's duel is an archetypal Egyptian battle primarily because he cannot resist concluding his description of the fight with a long description of the material benefits of the triumph, thus shifting the agenda away from the ideological virtues of honour, glory and heroism to the traditional economic bottom line.

The impact of war on an individual soldier is rarely found among the evidence discussed above, and thus is rarely noted by scholars. Although the military played a central role in the life, economy and culture of ancient Egypt, few texts or images refer directly to its full effect on the general soldier. Any evidence for economic or status-related benefits to an individual are limited to the relatively small elite group who were able to commission monuments to record their activities. Thus the surviving details of training, recruitment and death are the results of an accumulation of fragmentary sources.

Military recruitment and training

The issue of recruitment and training of Egyptian soldiers is a complex one. It is likely that in the Old Kingdom the army was little more than conscripted labour forming a specialized element of the wider conscription of corvée labour, used for major building works such as the pyramids. The 6th-Dynasty biography of Weni, from his tomb at Abydos, demonstrates that the army conscripted for campaigns against the 'sand-dwellers' was made up of men holding a variety of civilian titles. The early Middle Kingdom military sector probably functioned in a similar manner, with men conscripted from around the country to participate in campaigns in Nubia, as well as for work on royal building projects at other times of the year. By the 13th Dynasty there is evidence that the Middle Kingdom fortresses were staffed by full-time soldiers who were based there permanently and perhaps began to interact more frequently with the local indigenous populations, as opposed to the earlier rota system that seems to have been used for the fortress personnel of the 12th Dynasty.

In the New Kingdom there seems to have been a more ready supply of volunteers, whether through individuals inheriting the role of a family member, as in the case of Ahmose son of Ibana (who succeeded his father), or through the enrolment of so-called 'mercenary' ethnic groups such as the Canaanites, Nubians and Mycenaeans (see Chapter 6). It is likely, however that some form of conscription remained, since, although a small number of troops were based in garrisons abroad, fighting was still strictly seasonal. It is possible that each year a specific number of men were levied from the provinces, though it is worth considering to what degree voluntary service existed.

Despite the likely harsh realities of military life, the Egyptian army would have been a potentially lucrative career, particularly in the New Kingdom. An inscription in the tomb of Ahmose-pen-nekhbet at Elkab states that he was rewarded with the gold of valour, given male and female slaves and was given land as a result of his actions on the battlefield. Another 'biographical' text, in the Theban tomb of Amenemheb, states: 'I took thirteen Asiatics as prisoner of war, thirteen men; seven asses; thirteen bronze lances …then my lord gave me the gold of valour.' Although these texts are from a funerary context and are often thought to resemble personal lists of rewards, they also show the distribution of war booty as well as the issue of medal-style awards ('flies of valour'), actual surviving examples of which are known from contemporary tombs.

It has also been noted that many soldiers owned land. The Wilbour Papyrus, of the mid-20th Dynasty, shows the system of land tenure in several regions of Egypt. A large number of small landholders bear military titles varying from infantryman (*waw*), to charioteer (*kt*), and even foreign troops, such as the Sherden (see Chapter 6). There are also earlier instances of this kind of distribution of land to soldiers, with Ahmose son of Ibana, in the early 18th Dynasty, stating that his whole troop had been given land for their valiant actions. These texts indicate that any rank of the Egyptian military could be rewarded for their services.

Status and rank are also considered to have been important aspects of a military career in Egypt. Ahmose son of Ibana, describes himself as initially a *waw*, the lowest rank of the military, but his funerary texts suggest that he worked his way through the ranks to achieve the position of crew commander. Such promotion and career development were certainly possible in the Egyptian military sector; however, economic status at birth probably determined the potential progression of an individual. Chariotry was certainly a separate wing to the infantry, but it is not clear whether members of the infantry could be promoted to a position where a career with the chariotry was attainable. It is also difficult to know whether regular soldiers (i.e. those without elite connections) were able to attain high-ranking positions.

The nature of training in the early pharaonic period is difficult to determine, and it is not until the Middle Kingdom that the first evidence appears, in the 11th-Dynasty tomb of Baqet III (BH15) at Beni Hasan. On one wall of the tomb there are a series of registers depicting men wrestling, as well as a lower scene portraying what appears to be an actual battle. Similar scenes are found in the New Kingdom battle of Qadesh reliefs, in which Egyptian soldiers are shown practising military tactics and fighting. There is strong evidence that this training could be excruciating and harsh. A school exercise from Papyrus Anastasi III, also dating to the New Kingdom, describes a boy being inducted into the infantry, sent to a barracks for training, and experiencing harsh discipline, including beatings. A similar text, from Papyrus Anastasi I, shows that life after training was still difficult, stating the aftermath of a long march in the following way: 'you stop in the evening; with all of your body crushed and battered; your [limbs] are bruised'. Although these writings are a form of satire written from a scribal perspective during the 19th Dynasty, with the deliberate aim of castigating military life and instead promoting the lifestyle of a genteel bureaucrat, the description may have had some basis in real life, especially as troops marching to Asia would have had to walk through the hostile desert route of the 'Ways of Horus' in northern Sinai.

The instruction of New Kingdom soldiers, which probably took place in special military training camps, seems to have involved a combination of drill practice and regular physical punishment. The decoration in the Theban tomb of Userhet (TT 56), an army officer at the time of Amenhotep II, includes scenes of the reception of recruits, barbers cutting soldiers' hair, and quartermasters issuing rations. The tomb of Tjanuny (TT 74), an army scribe in the reign of Thutmose IV, contains similar scenes, including a magnificent depiction of five marching Nubian (probably Medjay) 'mercenaries' wearing long net-like kilts reinforced with leather and decorated with leopards' tails. One carries a military standard – a constant feature of Egyptian warfare since Protodynastic times – bearing a depiction of two wrestlers. Another scene in Tjanuny's tomb shows well-fed cattle being herded into the army camp as food for the troops.

Among Ramesses II's reliefs of the battle of Qadesh there are two (on the west wing of the Luxor temple pylon and on the north wall of the Great Temple at Abu Simbel) that include detailed depictions of the temporary camp set up by the Egyptian army on the move. The encamped soldiery, as well as stables for horses and cattle, are shown surrounded by a rectangular barricade of shields. In the centre of the camp was the royal pavilion, surrounded by the smaller rectangular-framed tents of the military hierarchy.

These images present a vivid and relatively congenial view of army life, whereas many of the literary texts of New Kingdom scribes, like Papyrus Lansing, already quoted above, were obviously designed to discourage the young from pursuing a military career. Papyrus Anastasi III presents a typically jaundiced outlook on army life:

> Come, I will describe to you the lot of the infantryman, the much exerted one: he is brought as a child of *nbi* and confined to a barrack. A painful blow is dealt to his body, a savage blow to his eye and a splitting blow to his brow. His head is split open with a wound. He is laid down

and beaten like a piece of papyrus. He is lambasted with beatings. Come, I will describe to you his journey to the land of Kharu and his march over the hills: his bread and water are carried on his shoulders like a donkey's burden. His neck becomes calloused, like a donkey's, and the arches of his back are bent. He drinks foul-tasting water and halts to stand guard. When he reaches the enemy he is like a pinioned bird, with no strength in his limbs. If he succeeds in returning to Egypt he is like a stick that the wood-worm has eaten – he is full of sickness. He is carried back in a state of paralysis on the back of a donkey. His clothes have been stolen and his retainer has run away.

Rewarding soldiers

Certainly the Egyptian soldier would have undergone enormous physical suffering both in training and in action, but the rich rewards of survival – in the form of personal advancement, spoils of war and gifts of land and livestock upon retirement from military service – would have been some compensation for the survivors of battles and campaigns. The 20th-Dynasty Wilbour Papyrus, mentioned above, is part of the evidence that the state provided for military veterans.

In the early New Kingdom there were important changes not only in the way that the army was organized, but in the role that it played in Egyptian society. On the basis of comparisons between the funerary inscriptions of the 6th-Dynasty official Weni at Abydos and the early 18th-Dynasty soldier Ahmose son of Ibana at Elkab, it has been suggested that there may have been no system of reward for individual soldiers in the Old Kingdom, and that complex systems of recompense might not have been introduced until after the Hyksos period (*c.*1550 BC onwards), possibly as a direct result of the adoption of Asiatic customs of warfare. Thus, the term *skr ʿnḫ* (literally, 'living captive') was used indiscriminately in the Old and Middle Kingdoms to refer both to enemies captured on the battlefield and to those taken while plundering defeated settlements, whereas from the late 18th Dynasty onwards it was used specifically to refer to enemy soldiers captured during the battle itself. The term *ḥȝḳt* was used to describe people or goods captured only in the course of post-battle plundering, taken to the king and then redistributed as rewards to individual soldiers, and finally the term ḥꜣḳ was used in the 18th Dynasty to designate both objects and people taken in the course of the actual battle and the subsequent plundering.

As with the weaponry, we should beware of suggesting that all changes that emerged in the early 18th Dynasty can be ascribed to contact with the Hyksos. It is equally likely – perhaps more likely – that the adoption of more complex systems of military recompense resulted from increasing Egyptian cultural and economic involvement in Syria-Palestine, and the consequent absorption of the 'language' of Asiatic warfare, just as the Egyptians clearly adopted Akkadian as the language of diplomacy by the middle of the 18th Dynasty.

Treatment of the injured and dead

The anthropological evidence for battle in Egypt stretches back at least as far as the 12th millennium BC when struggles between bands of Palaeolithic (Qadan culture, c.12,000 BP) hunter-gatherers led to flint arrowheads becoming embedded in the bones of almost half of the individuals buried in Cemetery 117 at Jebel Sahaba, near Wadi Halfa. A total of 59 human skeletons were excavated at Jebel Sahaba; each of them was in a semi-contracted position on the left side of the body, with the head to the east, facing south.

Out of the 59 individuals found at Cemetery 117, 24 showed signs of a violent death attested either by many chert points embedded in the bones (and even inside the skull) or by the presence of severe cut marks on the bones. The existence of multiple burials (including a group of up to eight bodies in one grave) seems to confirm the picture of violence. Since woman and children represent about 50% of this cemetery population, it is most probable that the Jebel Sahaba cemetery represents an exceptionally dramatic event. It has been suggested that a severe conflict of this kind may have been a consequence of the increasingly difficult conditions of living caused by unpredictable and catastrophic Nile floods, and the subsequent cutting down of the Nile into its former floodplain. A smaller cemetery, almost opposite Jebel Sahaba on the other side of the Nile, where such 'projectiles' were entirely absent from the bodies, shows that death was not always caused by violence at this date. However, some researchers have questioned whether the Jebel Sahaba evidence of hunter-gatherer conflict can be interpreted as resulting from a full-scale pitched battle, on the basis that the varied ages and sexes of the victims might be better explained by conditions of 'endemic raiding and ambush' rather than the effect of standard, organized warfare, since the latter would tend to have by far the highest impact on young to middle-aged adult males.

The ability to study injuries and possible cause of death in later Egyptian populations is sometimes hampered by the fact that 19th- and early 20th-century excavators in Egypt tended to leave a great deal of skeletal material behind when they excavated cemeteries, sometimes bringing back only the skulls. There has therefore been a disproportionate amount of research devoted to injuries to the head, as opposed to other parts of the body. Joyce Filer's study of Egyptian and Nubian human skulls from two sources (26th–30th-Dynasty graves at Giza and 12th–13th-Dynasty graves at Kerma) indicates that skeletal remains from a wide variety of sites and dates can provide intriguing evidence of the types of injuries inflicted on the battlefield; anthropological evidence of this type is an invaluable means of verifying and complementing the details of the surviving textual and pictorial descriptions of Egyptian battle.

Generally speaking, cranial injuries are found on the front and parietal sections of human skulls, thus probably indicating that the wounds resulted from face-to-face assaults. The tendency for such lesions to occur on the left side of skulls probably usually relates to the attacker being right-handed. Filer's earlier set of skulls, from Kerma, mainly consisted of 'oval and depressed head lesions', suggesting that the wounds were primarily inflicted by sticks, stones, maces and clubs. The Giza skulls, dating several centuries later, were characterized by a wide range of head injuries, including severe gashes and slicing incidents – these are generally suggestive of battle wounds inflicted by weapons of more advanced technology, such as daggers, swords, axes and crushing weapons.

In the late 19th century, the body of the 17th-Dynasty Theban king Seqenenra Tao II (c.1560 BC) was found, along with numerous New Kingdom royal mummies in western Thebes. His body is poorly preserved, with the skeleton mostly disarticulated and only

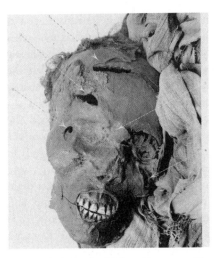

Mummified head of King Seqenenra Tao II of the Theban 17th Dynasty, c.1560 BC, showing multiple facial and cranial injuries. (G. Elliot Smith, The Royal Mummies, Cairo, 1912; Wikimedia)

part of the skin preserved. The skull was covered with traces of hideous wounds: a dagger thrust behind the ear; blows (perhaps inflicted by a mace) on cheek and nose; and a cut above the forehead, perhaps from an axe, and possibly matching the dimensions of a particular type of axe blade prevalent both in Syria-Palestine and in the eastern Delta of Egypt during the Hyksos period (c.1650–1550 BC).

Modern examinations of the king's body show that the cut above the ear might have been sustained earlier than the other wounds, as it had started to heal. This has in turn been suggested as a possible indication that the later wounds were inflicted in a successful assassination, since the initial wound above the ear could well have been sufficiently acute to prevent him from going into to battle. On the other hand, it has been pointed out that the body is poorly preserved, compared with other royal mummies, as a result of hasty embalming, which might tie in with rapid burial after battle. The autopsy of Seqenenra Tao II remains an interesting piece of evidence in relation to the general question as to whether Egyptian rulers genuinely played an active physical role in battle, as many texts and images seem to suggest, or whether the reality was more pragmatic and rather less heroic.

Medical analyses of battle scenes

As well as the anthropological data discussed above, there is a surprising amount of medical detail that can be deduced from the many images of battle portrayed particularly on New Kingdom temple walls (see Chapter 3). Gonzalo Sanchez, a neurosurgeon at the School of Medicine of the University of Dakota, has analysed a number of 19th and 20th-Dynasty battle reliefs, focusing specifically on the anatomical and medical details. Sanchez argues that the artists' depictions of wounded and dead soldiers in Ramesside battle scenes seem to be highly accurate from a medical point of view.

In the case of the battle of Qadesh, Sanchez quantified the soldiers directly involved in the battle using the scenes from the Luxor temple, the Ramesseum (mortuary temple of Ramesses II in western Thebes) and the Great Temple at Abu Simbel. Injuries were only found among the Hittites and their allies. In the two main tableaux depicting the battle of Qadesh, the so-called 'camp' and 'battle' scenes, Sanchez identified specific injuries on about 70% of the 63 Hittite charioteers shown breaking into the Egyptian military camp. He found that most of these injuries were inflicted from a frontal direction onto the upper body, suggesting that they derived from close combat rather than long-range weaponry, i.e. most (86–100%) of the injuries are to the upper body and 79–87% are inflicted from a frontal direction. According to Sanchez, one scene (portrayed at Abu Simbel) shows a Hittite, struck by an arrow on the top of his head, who displays classic symptoms of 'decerebrate rigidity', in that he is portrayed falling backwards, with his neck extended, his shoulders thrust forward, and his wrists limp.

In the main 'battle' tableau of the Qadesh scenes, Sanchez calculates that 282 Hittite or Syrian chariot corps were directly involved, and that the depictions were evidently designed to give the impression that most of their injuries were inflicted by Ramesses II himself, although most of the rest (about 28%) were caused by Egyptian charioteers. All of the versions show Hittites being killed beneath the wheels of Ramesses II's chariot, as well as some being drowned in Orontes, but, for some reason, the version of the battle portrayed in the Ramesseum temple shows the highest numbers of injured enemies (58%).

Generally speaking, the distribution of injuries across the bodies of dead and injured enemies in the 'battle' tableau ties in with bow-and-arrow conflict, the chest and abdomen being the most frequent target areas (80–90% of arrow injuries) while the rest are head and neck wounds (many of which have a high angle of impact, presumably designed to suggest that the king's arrows were responsible). The nature of the injuries suggests that the direction of attack is mostly frontal (e.g. 81% of attacks in the Luxor Temple reliefs), but Sanchez points out that that, as we view the scenes of the battle from the First to the Second Pylon of the Ramesseum, it is possible to construct a continuous narrative of different stages of the battle, culminating in Ramesses II's pursuit of retreating Hittites in the latter stages of battle (which clearly necessarily involves increasing numbers of injuries perpetrated from behind).

Disposing of the dead?

In 1923 a mass-grave of at least sixty men was excavated by Herbert Winlock of the Metropolitan Museum, New York, near the tomb of the 11th-Dynasty ruler Nebhepetra Mentuhotep II in western Thebes. Partly because of damage by tomb-robbers, only ten complete skeletons had survived, but the estimate of a minimum of 60 individuals was based on the survival of 59 skulls and 52 right femurs. Average age at death across the whole group was estimated at 30–40 years old on the basis of teeth abrasion.

Many of the individuals have been diagnosed as suffering from severe head-wounds that were assumed to have been sustained in the course of siege warfare, and in one case an ebony-tipped arrow-head was discovered still embedded in an eye socket. There were also a number of fractures of forearms suggesting that some of the dead had been fending off attack with close combat weapons shortly before death. Five wrist-guards (typically worn by archers) were also found in the tomb. Four of the men had wounds that had already healed before death (indicative of their having lived violent, perhaps military, lives), and six appeared to have been savaged by vultures, strongly suggesting a probable period in which their bodies lay exposed in the aftermath of battle. In slight contradiction to the damage from vultures, a number of the bodies had been bandaged during rigor mortis, which can begin as quickly as one hour after death. In many cases the bodies were also covered with thick layers of sand – a circumstance that was somewhat more difficult to explain or interpret.

The un-embalmed, linen-wrapped bodies of these men, almost certainly killed in battle, and subsequently placed together in a rock-cut common tomb, were preserved by dehydration – therefore, despite the absence of any embalming, these corpses are the best-preserved of all Middle Kingdom bodies. Because they were buried as a group and within sight of the royal cemetery, it was surmised that they had died in some particularly heroic conflict. Winlock suggested, more specifically, that they had died in the civil war between Thebes and Herakleopolis, which concluded with Theban victory during Mentuhotep II's reign.

Winlock's argument that the men died while besieging Herakleopolis was based very much on the acute angles at which most of the arrows could be seen to have entered the bodies; this was interpreted as evidence that the bows were being fired from parapets and battlements above the besieging force. More recently, however, Carola Vogel has pointed out that such arrow wounds could just as easily result from bowmen releasing their arrows in formation at a 45-degree angle on an open battlefield – this is something that they could well have done to avoid hitting fellow soldiers and optimize their range. It has been pointed out that there are depictions of archers in the battle reliefs of Seti I releasing their arrows typically at just such a 45-degree angle.

Additionally Winlock had argued that these were 11th-Dynasty soldiers (and therefore contemporary with the Thebes–Herakleopolis civil war) primarily on the basis that their mass-grave MMA 507 was located in the middle of a row of early Middle Kingdom elite graves, close to the tomb of Mentuhotep II. Now, however, this early dating has been questioned, partly because hieratic labels on some of the linen bandaging perhaps date to the 12th or 13th Dynasty, and partly because the arrowheads and wrist-guards could actually date to any time during the Middle Kingdom. A later date now seems more likely (e.g. the early 12th-Dynasty reigns of Amenemhat I or Senusret I), and it now also seems much less likely that they died in siege warfare at Herakleopolis. They nevertheless represent clear evidence of the types of fatal injuries sustained by Egyptian soldiers in Middle Kingdom warfare.

Whatever the answer as to the battlefield where the soldiers buried at Deir el-Bahari actually met their fate, this debate does raise the issue of the extent to which the Egyptians may ever have sought to repatriate individuals either from foreign lands or simply from other parts of Egypt, to give them a proper burial in their home cemetery (bearing in mind the clear importance of funerary rites and mummification in Egyptian culture). One answer to this is provided by the funerary inscription in the tomb of Pepynakht, a provincial governor in the 6th-Dynasty reign of Pepy II (*c.*2278–2184 BC), at Aswan. As his inscription indicates, Pepynakht (also known as Heqaib) was sent to bring back the body of a colleague who had died while commissioning a boat in Western Asia (see Chapter 7 below):

> So his majesty sent me to the land of the Aamu (Asiatics), so as to bring back (the body of) the "sole companion", controller of Nekhen, the overseer of foreigners, Anankhta son of Kaaper, who was assembling a *kbnt*-boat there in order to travel to Punt, when the Aamu and the dwellers-on-the-sands (bedouin) killed him together with the armed detachment which was accompanying him.

That the text only refers to the retrieval of the corpse of Anankhta himself, and therefore the evident abandonment of the bodies of the whole group of soldiers that had died with him, suggests that on the rare occasions that such repatriation took place, it was reserved for the elite.

Treating the injured

Although we have no really specific surviving texts or images in relation to the way that Egyptians treated those who were injured in battle, there are a number of documents that do give some indication of the medical techniques that may have been available. A number of surviving papyri (fourteen relatively complete examples and several fragments) provide information concerning the Egyptians' knowledge of healing and the nature of the human body. The 18th-Dynasty Edwin Smith Medical Papyrus (New York Academy of Medicine; *c.*1600 BC) was perhaps the work of a military surgeon, in which case it may have served as a kind of textbook of the treatment of different kinds of trauma suffered in battle. It has also been suggested, however, that its author may have been a doctor associated with a workforce concerned with stone masonry construction.

The papyrus deals mainly with such problems as broken bones, dislocations and crushings, dividing its 48 cases into three classes: 'an ailment which I will treat', 'an ailment with which I will contend' and 'an ailment not to be treated'. The symptoms of each case are described and, where possible, a remedy prescribed. The majority of the problems are traumatic head and upper limb injuries (topographically ordered from the skull, neck, upper limbs and chest down to the thoracolumbar spine). Since the text ends very abruptly, mid-sentence, it seems likely that the writer (or writers) was about to write down more cases dealing with wounds and injuries to the thoracolumbar spine, sacrum and lower limbs. About 13 out of the 48 injuries appear to relate to some kind of gaping incision wound that could have been created by a cutting weapon such as an axe, knife or *khepesh* sword (see Chapter 5).

The wider medical significance of the Edwin Smith Papyrus is also worth noting. The treatments prescribed for a variety of spinal injuries are regarded as good rational procedures even compared with modern medical practice in these cases. The writer of the papyrus already appears to be effectively distinguishing 'vertebral body compression fractures' from 'vertebral body burst fractures', many millennia before they were categorized in the 20th century through Watson–Jones's vertebral body fracture classification. Although it cannot be claimed that the Edwin Smith Papyrus writer fully understood the concept of the circulation of the blood, he clearly recognized that the condition of the heart could be judged by the pulse:

> The counting of anything with the fingers [is done] to recognize the way the heart goes. There are vessels in it leading to every part of the body . . . When a Sekhmet priest, any *swnw* doctor . . . puts his fingers to the head . . . to the two hands, to the place of the heart . . . it speaks . . . in every vessel, every part of the body.

This level of knowledge concerning blood circulation is also suggested by another medical text that was found in the same tomb: the Ebers Papyrus.

Defining images of warfare

In modern times, photographers invariably provide images of front-line action in war-zones, and the photographs of Vietnam, Cambodia and the Gulf wars often become part of the folk memory of these events – in the case of the first Gulf War, in 1991, for instance, a shot of an Iraqi soldier who had burned to death in an armoured vehicle served as a particularly bleak defining image of the war's closing stages. In World War I, Otto Dix the German painter was one of the young men conscripted into the conflict – while fighting as an infantry-man between 1915 and 1918 he produced numerous sketches, including some showing scenes in the battle of the Somme. Years after Dix had produced a series of anti-war prints from these sketches, an unknown Second World War soldier wrote a letter home describing the impact that Dix's prints had had on him, and how he felt about them now that he was at war himself:

> I've forgotten the artist's name. But his pictures won't let me alone. One of a wounded soldier, gazing into emptiness like a madman; another of a ghastly mining landscape. A sketch of ripped-up earth like where we lie at the moment.

We can rarely, if ever, expect to find such overt and expressive anti-war sentiments in Egyptian texts or images relating to battle, but we can at least occasionally gain a sense of the individual alone in the misery of the foreign campaign. In the depiction of Ramesses II's army encamped near Qadesh, there are a number of more intimate glimpses, such as the scene of a soldier holding his head in his hands, and another showing the tending of a soldier's leg-wound.

CHAPTER 5

—————————

WEAPONRY AND TACTICS

This chapter not only describes the evidence for weaponry typically used by Egyptians at different dates, but also discusses the ways in which the types of military equipment and battle strategy need to be seen as parts of a complex and symbiotic process. Sometimes particular military strategies are sparked off by the acquisition of new types of weapons, and sometimes the adoption of new methods of warfare can result in the emergence of weapons that can enhance and facilitate such methods. It is therefore necessary to examine the ways in which types of tactics and weaponry ebbed and flowed between different armies and states rather than being fixed components of ethnically, culturally or territorially defined groups. This has repercussions for our approach to the study of ancient weaponry, the technology and dissemination of which may not have been so clearly delineated by cultural and ethnic boundaries as we have previously assumed.

Weapons used at different dates

Weaponry was a crucial and well-attested area of Egyptian material culture, sometimes surviving among elite funerary equipment, and also (although much less frequently) found in settlement contexts. The analysis of this material suggests that Egyptian weaponry was very often similar – and occasionally identical – to weapons used by inhabitants of neighbouring regions, especially those of Western Asia. These similarities in weaponry are usually assumed to result from Egyptian adoption of technology derived from neighbouring cultures.

With the development of a professional army it is believed that the Egyptian weapons 'industry' became the business of the government, with military workshops initially attached to the temples, but later transferring to the royal treasury and military headquarters in the Ramesside period. The weapons industry would have been very large, needing to supply thousands of troops, and would have required significant resources. Egyptians employed a standard repertoire of weapons throughout the dynastic period, the main types being the spear, javelin, bow and arrow, and, in the New Kingdom, swords and chariots. The mace (discussed in Chapter 2) was used from the Neolithic period through to the end of the Early Dynastic period, although it had probably become a largely ceremonial item by the 1st Dynasty.

A core set of materials were essential for the production of weapons in the dynastic period: namely, wood, leather, stone and copper alloy. Copper-tin alloy (i.e. bronze) was only used occasionally throughout the Old and Middle Kingdoms, due to a dearth of tin in Egypt. Chemical analyses of Egyptian axes have shown that arsenical copper was employed as a deliberate alloy from an early period, with tin-based bronzes being used only on a limited scale. This dependence on arsenic alloys would not have produced such strong weapons, but it would at least have allowed the Egyptians to make more productive use of copper.

The spear was the main short-range weapon used in Egypt throughout the Dynastic period. The earliest examples are depicted on the Protodynastic 'Hunters' Palette'(British Museum, EA20790, c.3200 BC) – from this source it can be seen that the spear of the late 4th millennium BC consisted of a long staff and a leaf-shaped blade with protuberant spine. In the Old and Middle kingdoms, spear-heads (usually flint or copper) were attached to the wooden staff by a 'tang' carved as an integral part of the blade. Spears were being manufactured in the Middle Kingdom fortress of Mirgissa, judging from the excavation of about three hundred flint spear-heads at this site. The use of copper alloy for spear-heads at about the same date, however, is attested by a wooden model from the 11th-Dynasty tomb of Mesehti (discussed in Chapter 1), which represents forty Egyptian spearmen, each carrying a spear consisting of a bronze blade set on

Detail of the Hunters' Palette, showing three Protodynastic warriors carrying various weapons, including a throwstick, a mace, two spears, and a bow and arrow, c.3200 BC (British Museum). (Paul Vyse)

a long wooden shaft. These two different types of evidence not only show the simultaneous use of different materials for parts of the same weapon type, but probably also reflect the difference between the ideal (bronze depicted in a tomb model) and the normal physical reality (use of flint at a military barracks). In the New Kingdom, bronze seems to have become more readily available for spear-heads; this increased use of copper alloy (at the same time as evidence for a considerable increase in contact with Western Asia) is believed to be a crucial factor in a change to socketed spear-heads rather than the previously utilized method of connecting to the staff by a tang, which was clearly more suited to stone spear-heads. Whereas the conventional spear was intended to be thrown at the enemy, there was also a form of halberd, which was effectively a spear shaft fitted with an axe blade and used for cutting and slashing.

Axes and daggers were depicted frequently in tomb and temple decoration, and many examples have also been found in archaeological contexts. In the Old and Middle Kingdoms the conventional axe usually consisted of a semi-circular copper head (A) tied to a wooden handle by cords, threaded through perforations in the copper, and wrapped around lugs. At this stage there was little difference between the battle axe and the woodworker's axe. In the Middle Kingdom, however, some battle axes had longer blades with concave sides narrowing down to a curved edge (B). The Egyptians

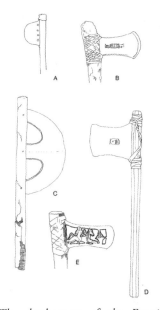

The development of the Egyptian battle-axe from (A) semi-circular axe (Old and Middle Kingdom), (B) long axe (Middle Kingdom), (C) three-tanged 'epsilon' axe (Middle Kingdom), (D) long, narrow axe (New Kingdom), and (E) openwork axe (New Kingdom).

more commonly used the tang-style cutting axe rather than the socketed axe found primarily in Western Asia. A particularly common axe in Egypt was the three-tanged epsilon axe, which was frequently used in battle during the Middle Kingdom; it was manufactured with three tangs wedged into grooves in a spear-style haft, and secured with cord (C). 'Duck-bill' axes were also common in this period, and are clearly depicted in the tomb of Khnumhotep II at Beni Hasan (BH3); this type of axe remained in use during the Second Intermediate Period when more rounded forms were developed, before being replaced by a splayed variety, with straight or incurved sides, that became predominant in the New Kingdom. This change is believed to have been adopted to improve the axe's ability to penetrate the target. The design is also widely regarded as linked to the development of body armour. The axe remained an important weapon up to the end of the 18th Dynasty, until it was gradually supplanted by the sickle sword (or *khepesh*, see below).

The dagger, typically made from copper alloy, retained roughly the same design throughout the majority of the Bronze Age. From the Middle Kingdom onwards, it grew in popularity as a weapon for stabbing and crushing at close quarters. The two edged-blade, which, prior to the New Kingdom, was usually riveted to a bone or ivory handle, was sometimes decorated with grooves in the form

Middle Kingdom three-tanged 'epsilon' battle axe, comprising the original copper alloy blade, but restored wooden handle and lashing, unprovenanced, c.1980–1800 BC (New York: Metropolitan Museum of Art 15.2.5a). (MMA Open Content Program)

of plants or birds. More sophisticated production techniques were introduced in the New Kingdom, facilitating production of a narrower, sharper blade.

A variety of swords have been found in 19th- and 20th-Dynasty contexts, although the real physical extent of their use is difficult to determine, since the few surviving examples derive from funerary assemblages. By the beginning of the New Kingdom in Egypt many new types of weaponry had been introduced from Western Asia, including such crucial items as the chariot and the composite bow (see below). It was in this context of rapid military innovation and change that a new form of dagger appeared; with its narrow blade and tang cast all in one, it gradually developed into a weapon resembling a short sword. The most specialized form of sword was the *khepesh* (ḫpš), a scimitar-like weapon with a curved blade modelled on an Asiatic form that first appeared in the Middle Bronze Age and is also known as a 'curved sword' or 'sickle sword'. The sharpened edge of the *khepesh* was on the inside of the curvature, making it particularly useful for hacking motions. The manufacturing techniques required to produce this weapon were probably adopted from Middle Bronze Age Syria-Palestine; however, direct imports of this weapon, through trade or tribute, may also have occurred, as the example found in the tomb of Tutankhamun demonstrates. The first Egyptian textual reference to a *khepesh* sword occurs in one of the stelae erected by the 17th-Dynasty ruler Kamose in Karnak temple, c.1550 BC, and the first image of the sickle sword in an Egyptian context appears in the tomb of Menkheperrasoneb, dating

Middle Kingdom (or perhaps early New Kingdom) copper alloy duckbill axe, h. 5.1cm, w. 10.9cm, c.1980–1500 BC (New York: Metropolitan Museum of Art 41.6.9). (MMA Open Content Program)

to the reign of Thutmose III (*c.* 1479–1425 BC) where it forms part of a scene of items of tribute arriving into the Egyptian court from Syria.

The *khepesh* – averaging between 40 and 65 cm in length – was widely used by the Egyptian army in the 19th Dynasty, when it is frequently depicted in the hands of soldiers at the battle of Qadesh (*c.*1274 BC). The northern exterior wall of the 20th-Dynasty mortuary temple of Ramesses III (Medinet Habu) is decorated with episodes from the war against the Sea Peoples (*c.*1164 BC), including a scene showing *khepesh* swords and various other weapons being allocated to the soldiers. This type of sword is also frequently featured as the principal hand-weapon wielded by Ramesside rulers in royal smiting and chariot scenes. In the smiting scenes it usually replaces the mace (see Chapter 2) as the favoured weapon in scenes of royal victory and domination. Some depictions, such as those on two of the temple pylons at Karnak, show the sword being ceremonially presented to the king by the gods Amun or Montu. This ritual link is no doubt connected with the fact that the shape of the sword resembles the foreleg of an ox, which the Egyptians also knew as *khepesh*. Decoration

Copper alloy Egyptian dagger with ivory handle, unprovenanced but dated stylistically to the 17th or 18th Dynasty, l. 30.8cm, c.1600–1500 BC (New York: Metropolitan Museum of Art 40.2.7). (MMA Open Content Program)

in the interior of the chariot of Thutmose IV (Cairo, Egyptian Museum CG46097) shows Montu presenting a *khepesh* sword to the king and stating, 'I have given to you the *khepesh* and bravery in order to trample the bowmen in their places.'

The Liverpool 'khepesh' sword The Liverpool *khepesh* sword is unprovenanced but it is likely to be from a funerary context, both because it was probably excavated by John Garstang – whose Egyptian work focused largely on cemeteries – and because most other surviving examples appear to come from tombs, as in the case of the two from the funerary equipment of Tutankhamun (Cairo Egyptian Museum). It has been suggested that the Liverpool example may date to the early 19th Dynasty since there is a very similar *khepesh* from Mesopotamia, inscribed in cuneiform with the name of the Assyrian ruler Adad-Nirari I (reg. c. 1307 – 1275 BC; New York, Metropolitan Museum, II.166.I[472]). This not only helps with the dating but also demonstrates that a sword of this type, like the chariot or the composite bow, was very much an international weapon of the late Bronze Age.

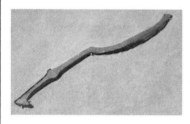

Khepesh sword, 19th Dynasty, l.57.8cm, (in Garstang Museum, University of Liverpool).

Although the Liverpool *khepesh*, like other surviving examples of this date, was cast all in one piece, it comprises three basic components: the handle, the curved scimitar-like blade, and the forte (a straight section between the handle and the blade). The handle has a 3 mm deep recess in it, presumably intended to take ivory inlay, as in the case of one of Tutankhamun's swords, which still preserves some traces of ivory. The end of the blade is squared off rather than pointed, suggesting that it was used for slashing rather than stabbing.

The emergence of archery

The bow and arrow (or *pesedjet*) was the basic long-range weapon in Egypt from the outset of the pharaonic period. Along with plaited slings, bows provided a means of long-range assault that could back up hand-to-hand fighting with slashing and stabbing weapons.

In the late Predynastic Period the 'horn bow' was in common use; this consisted of a pair of oryx or antelope horns connected by a central piece of wood. It is the earliest instance of a type of bow sometimes described as the 'double curved decurve' type. Despite the relative frequency of the depiction of this type of bow in late Predynastic art, for example on the Hunters' Palette, dating to *c.*3200 BC (mentioned above in relation to early images of spears), only a very few physical examples have survived. Some fragments of 1st-Dynasty horn bows, as well as numerous ivory and wooden arrow-heads (some with their tips stained with iron oxide, perhaps as poison), were excavated by Flinders Petrie from the royal tombs of Djer and Den in the Umm el-Qa'ab area of Abydos (Oxford, Pitt Rivers Museum 1901.40.43.1-5; Cairo, Egyptian Museum, JE34981). Another horn bow from the Abydos royal tombs is in the collection of the Berlin Museum (Accession No. 18041), although it has no records linking it with any specific tomb at the site. Finally, part of a 1st-Dynasty horn bow was excavated from Tarkhan tomb 22, but its current whereabouts are unknown.

By the pharaonic period, Egyptian archers were most commonly depicted using a 'self' or 'simple' bow (also sometimes described as a 'single-staved' bow), typically made from acacia or sidder (Christ's Thorn) wood, and firing reed or wooden arrows. Twenty-two wooden self bows have so far been identified; thirteen of these are made from acacia (*A. nilotica*), six from Christ's Thorn (or sidder-wood; *Ziziphus spina-Christi*), and three from tamarisk (*Tamarix aphylla*). It is almost certainly the greater elasticity of acacia that caused it to be preferred over the other two wood types. The earliest known surviving actual example of an Egyptian self bow is an Early Dynastic example from the site of Tarkhan (Manchester Museum 5433), which is usually described as a 'segment' form of self bow (i.e. the profile of the wood forms a single distinctive gentle curve).

The self bow, mostly measuring between 1 and 2 metres in length, was produced from a stave of nearly straight wood, trimmed at each end to produce a tapered effect, and strung with twisted gut. Longer self bows, often strengthened at certain points by binding with cord, tended to be either straighter than before or 'recurved'. The recurved bow, which consisted of two convex sections, had greater power and range. Physical examples of self bows have survived from the New Kingdom, but visual images of earlier examples have survived in several tombs, including scenes in the tomb of Khnumhotep II at Beni Hasan, and the model of forty Nubian archers from the tomb of Mesehti at Asyut, already mentioned above. Various different profiles/shapes of self bow were created in Egypt and elsewhere. The specific profile of a bow determines the amount of energy that can be stored in its limbs. The more 'work' that the bow limbs need to undertake when a bow is drawn, the more energy is stored within them, and therefore the faster the speed at which the arrow can move, once released.

The wood used for self bows needed to bend without breaking, and this seems to have been achieved by steaming the wood to increase pliability during the manufacturing process. There are scenes in the tombs of Amenemhat and Baqt II at Beni Hasan (BH2 and BH15) showing steam-bending being used for the manufacture of bows. In both scenes, the craftsmen are shown first holding wood over a pot of hot water to allow the steam to penetrate and soften the cellular structure, and secondly actually bending the stick into a hoop shape, with the ends buried in the ground to keep the shape.

The methods and materials used for production of the self bow appear to have changed very little throughout the pharaonic period, and the examples found in the tomb of Tutankhamun (*c.*1336–1327 BC) are likely to have been produced in the manner noted above. These bows are very unusual in retaining the remains of the bow-string (made from animal gut), still attached to the notches. The elasticity and ready availability of animal products such as sinews and gut would have made them perfect for the manufacture of bow-strings.

Scene in the 12th-Dynasty tomb of Amenemhat at Beni Hasan (BH2) showing steam-bending being used for the manufacture of bows, c.1965–1920 BC. (Paul Vyse, after Newberry 1893: pl.XI)

The introduction of the composite bow was part of a striking change in military equipment that occurred at the beginning of the New Kingdom. This modernization of the Egyptian army is usually attributed to the need to keep pace with the military innovations of neighbouring countries and prevent any reoccurrence of a Hyksos-style domination by foreigners, as had happened in the Second Intermediate Period. The composite bow was made from a combination of materials (essentially strips of horn and sinew glued to a wooden self bow), thus producing a stronger, more elastic and more effective weapon; it came in two types – recurved and triangular – and had a considerably greater range than the self bow. The main advantage of composite bows over self bows was their combination of smaller size with higher power, making them automatically more convenient than self bows in situations where the archer was mobile (e.g. on horseback or in a chariot).

Almost all composite bows are also recurve bows (i.e. the shape of the bow curves away from the archer), giving higher draw-weight in the early stages of the archer's draw, and thus maximizing total energy for a given final draw-weight. The kinetic energy required to deliver acceleration to an arrow is determined by the draw work of the archer versus the elasticity of the bow. The composite bow typically seems to have had a 40 lb (18 kg) draw, an average range of 100–180 metres. This can be compared with modern compound bows, which have a maximum draw of around 70 lb (32 kg) and an (accurate) range of about 40 metres.

The arrow shaft had to be made of a light, straight material, usually reed or wood, and most arrow-heads were made from bone, ivory, wood, metal or flint. Egyptian arrows have been found with or without fletching feathers at the end of the reed, although the addition of such a material clearly provided both accuracy and greater stability, and thus was probably widely utilized. From the study of Egyptian ballistics it is clear that the arrows could be delivered with impressive force from the new style of bow, in some cases allowing them to penetrate thick bone, including the skull. With the increased use of the composite bow and bronze arrowhead from the New Kingdom onwards, archery could pose an even more significant threat to opposing armies.

Changes in archery technology

Many innovations in Egyptian warfare seem to coincide with the immediate aftermath of the 'Hyksos period', in the mid-2nd

Scene in a military workshop showing a craftsman checking the straightness of an arrow, from an unidentified New Kingdom tomb at Saqqara.

millennium BC. It is often difficult to determine the extent to which each of these changes and innovations are linked in any causal way. From the point of view of the overall process of military change, the adoption of both chariots and composite bows must have been very closely linked, given that there is general agreement that chariots served above all as highly mobile bases from which archers could pick off the enemy from a distance (see detailed discussion of chariotry below).

As noted above, acacia wood was often used for self bows and their arrows, but the emergence of the composite bow led to a demand for different woods, including ash and birch. The only known specimens of ash from ancient Egypt are, firstly, a composite bow from the tomb of Tutankhamun (identified as *Fraxinus excelsior*), and, secondly, the axle, felloes and part of the frame of the floor of the so-called Florence chariot, which is usually dated to the mid-18th Dynasty, just a little earlier than the reign of Tutankhamun. Neither ash nor birch occur naturally in Egypt and both of these imports were used primarily for the creation and embellishment of chariots and composite bows. Although presumably most horn used in Egypt was derived from native – or at any rate African – species, some circumstantial evidence exists to suggest that the horns of the Cretan wild goat (*agrimi*) might have been imported for making Egyptian composite bows.

The introduction of the composite bow coincided with – and perhaps directly influenced – changes in the form of arm-guards and quivers. New types of arm-guards were introduced in the early New Kingdom, almost certainly because of the increasing use of the composite bow. Depictions of the brightly coloured arm-guards show them tied at both wrist and elbow. Unlike earlier guards, they cover much of the lower arm, but no actual examples seem to have survived, perhaps because they were made of something that would not have preserved well, such as padded textile.

During the New Kingdom, the typical tubular Middle Kingdom style of quiver began to be replaced by tapered, round-bottomed quivers that appear to have been better suited to chariotry warfare. The new style of quiver was almost certainly the result of a change in the status of bowman and the need for both archers and their equipment to be incorporated into the design of the chariot. The arrow and javelin quivers were attached to the side-panel of the chariot in such a way and at such a precise angle that the charioteer could easily remove an arrow or javelin from the quivers when needed.

Some well-preserved examples of New Kingdom quivers have survived. These were usually made from leather, occasionally utilizing complete animal skins. The funerary equipment in the 18th-Dynasty tomb of the royal standard-bearer Maiherpri in the Valley of the Kings (KV36, reign of Thutmose III, c.1450 BC) included two leather quivers, 75 reed arrows, and two leather arm-guards (all now in the Egyptian Museum, Cairo); both Maiherpri quivers still retain much of their well-crafted coloured decoration, one purely in appliqué style and the other also including raised relief motifs that appear to have been block-stamped into the leather. Tutankhamun's tomb included ten fragments of embossed gold sheet that probably derive either from quivers or bow-cases. An unprovenanced red leather quiver in the Ägyptisches Museum, Berlin, although subject to severe decay, can nevertheless be seen to have had intricate decoration, including open-work appliqués and couchwork with panels of superimposed multi-coloured strips and green, pinked edgings.

By the early New Kingdom, body armour had been introduced for Egyptian soldiers, comprising small bronze plates riveted to linen or leather jerkins. At around the same time, a smaller type of shield, with a tapered lower half, began to be used. Both the armour and new types of shields were surely also connected with the new requirement to protect soldiers against attack with composite bows. The above discussion of the complex interactions between such significantly innovative equipment as chariots, archery equipment, armour and shields indicates the tendency for weapons to operate as parts of organic, constantly changing tactical systems. Thus, particular items of military technology interact both with one another and with the tactical systems in which they are used. Cause and effect can often be difficult to disentangle, with regard to technology and strategy. Did military tactics change radically because of the increasing use of chariots, composite bows and other innovative weapons, or did these technological advances emerge at least partly in response to new kinds of military strategies?

The adoption of chariots by the Egyptian army

The Egyptian chariot appeared as part of a process of military modernization at the beginning of the New Kingdom. The Egyptians gained their knowledge of this technology from Canaan; therefore, their principal terms for chariot (*wrryt, mrkbt* and *tprt*) and for spans of chariot horses (*ḥtri*) were Asiatic loan-words. Early 18th-Dynasty Egyptian chariots appear to have been very similar to contemporary Canaanite vehicles, as demonstrated by the 'Florence chariot', a well-preserved surviving example dated to a little earlier than the reign of Tutankhamun (now in the collection of the National Archaeological Museum, Florence). The chariot was of particular use to the Egyptians for its speed, as the vehicle could be utilized as a mobile platform for an archer, who would deliver harassing fire against the enemy infantry. Ramesses II's accounts of the battle of Qadesh suggest that chariots could also be used tactically to mount surprise attacks involving the outflanking of enemy infantry while it was on the march. In the aftermath of battle, it is clear from texts and images that chariots could be used to transport living prisoners and the severed hands of enemy dead. Amenhotep II, for instance, is said to have brought back 16 Mitannian prisoners, attached to the side of his chariot, with another inside the chariot, and also 20 severed hands hanging from his horses' heads – although the physical logistics of this, for a standard Egyptian light chariot, seem to be rather formidable.

The accounts of the battles of Megiddo and Qadesh imply that the Egyptians and their Mitannian and Hittite opponents were each deploying several thousands of chariots, and indeed the Egyptian Megiddo booty lists claim that 924 chariots and 2041 horses were brought back as booty after that campaign. In reality, any numbers quoted in ancient texts need to be treated with extreme caution, and it is more likely that the numbers of chariots in the Egyptian army were much smaller, with perhaps a maximum of around two hundred operational vehicles at any one time in the New Kingdom, although any such estimates are highly tenuous. In contrast, contemporary infantry forces are normally estimated at several thousands.

The Egyptian chariot's generally light structure would have restricted its use. Early scholars wrongly saw its role as something like that of the modern tank or armoured vehicle but there is now a strong consensus that it was not used directly against opposing chariots, as it could have been comparatively easily destroyed in close combat, and was also probably of limited use in siege operations. It also could not be used on mountainous terrain and could easily be disabled with a simple spear attack. It therefore seems likely that, even after the introduction of the chariot, Egyptian infantry in practice continued to play key roles in the campaigns, and it is very difficult now to calculate just how prominent a role was played by chariotry. It is worth noting that the chariot was closely associated with elite presentation, and that this is probably a major reason why chariotry-based warfare has survived better in the visual record.

Two Egyptian soldiers in a chariot, portrayed as part of the depiction of the battle of Qadesh on the external walls of the Temple of Ramesses II at Abydos, c.1250 BC. (Paul Vyse)

Egyptian chariots, chariot forces and their production are all depicted in funerary contexts, as well as on temple walls, and the physical remains of around a dozen chariots have primarily survived from royal funerary contexts, such as those from the tombs of Tutankhamun, Yuya and Tuyu, Thutmose IV and Amenhotep II (just a fragmentary wheel in the case of the latter). Most surviving examples are incomplete, apart from the six well-known Tutankhamun chariots and a complete example in the Egyptian Museum, Florence, which was excavated in the 19th century from an unknown non-royal elite tomb in western Thebes. Additionally, some Late Bronze Age chariot parts were found outside Egypt, in the course of excavations at the Syro-Palestinian sites of Megiddo and Beth Shan (and also early Iron Age Philistine examples at Ashkelon and Ekron). Numerous small chariot components were also revealed during excavations in the 1990s at Qantir, the site of the Ramesside city of Piramesse, which included important military zones, where chariotry and horses were housed, as well as large areas of workshops producing weaponry.

The so-called Tano Chariot (comprising around sixty large pieces of leather in the Egyptian Museum, Cairo) is highly unusual in that it has survived purely in the form of the leather casing accoutrements, including not only casing from the chariot itself but also such related equipment as bow-cases, quivers, wrist-guards and parts of the horses' harnesses. The Tano Chariot is unprovenanced (having been purchased from the Tano family of antiquities dealers); therefore, it is unclear whether it derives from a tomb or workshop context (although the former is thought more likely). It has been dated, primarily on the basis of technological details, to c.1350–1100 BC. Ironically it is the leather casing that is most commonly missing from the other surviving chariots, although some chariot leather was found in the tombs of Amenhotep II, Thutmose IV, Amenhotep III and Tutankhamun.

The six chariots from the tomb of Tutankhamun are particularly helpful in determining the manufacturing process. The lower part of the vehicle was typically composed of two four-spoke wheels with the axle set towards the rear, and the chariot pole running beneath the centre of the vehicle floor, attached to the axle. The cart of the chariot would be positioned above the axle, allowing two passengers to stand. These components would all be produced from wood and held together using leather, rawhide and glue. Leather straps were added to the wheel to help hold it together and provide some cushioning between the ground and the wooden wheel, and rawhide was used to strengthen joints, wheel hubs, and as a bearing for the axle. Such regular use of glue and rawhide could only have been possible in a dry climate such as that of Egypt. Even so, frequent protection of joints with waterproof coverings, such as birch bark, indicates that the loosening of joints due to moisture may still have posed a problem.

The chariots of the New Kingdom, including the examples from Tutankhamun's tomb, are thought to stand technologically somewhere between the experimental Levantine examples of the 18th–17th centuries BC and the heavier type of the 1st millennium BC, shown in Assyrian reliefs. The New Kingdom Egyptian chariot, designed for speed, lightness and stability, is probably among the most sophisticated ever made, not just in terms of its decoration, but also in the technology involved in its construction.

When did chariotry first begin to be used by Egyptians? It is almost certain that the chariot was not invented in Egypt but introduced from the outside world, most likely from Western Asia. It was perhaps only during the reigns of Kamose and Ahmose (late 17th- to early 18th-Dynasty) that spoked wheels began to be used in Egypt; a small model carriage with the first known instances of Egyptian spoked wheels was discovered among the funerary equipment in the Theban tomb of Ahhotpe, mother of Ahmose. It was once frequently asserted that the chariot was introduced into Egypt by the Hyksos, but many scholars now believe that both Egyptians and Hyksos began to use it towards the end of the Second Intermediate Period (c. 1550 BC).

The adoption of any technological innovation tends to require a whole set of social and technological factors to fall into place and a suitable social or economic context within which the technology can flourish. In the case of Egyptian chariots, therefore, it was necessary to obtain certain raw materials (e.g. particular imported woods) and horses (not indigenous to Egypt). They also needed to gain access to specialized craftsmen and individuals with the necessary skills to use chariots effectively in battle, not to mention the adoption of military tactics that maximized the benefits of chariot corps.

The groups of workers producing chariots must have comprised one of the most complex of all ancient workshops, both because of the diversity of materials involved and the wide range of technological skills required. Several New Kingdom tombs show groups of craftsmen, such as carpenters, joiners and leather-workers working on the different parts of a chariot. One of the latest depictions of the manufacture of a chariot has been found in a 26th-Dynasty tomb at Saqqara, dating to the 6th or 7th century BC.

The principal materials used for a high-quality chariot were wood, leather, rawhide, textile, bone, ivory, copper alloy, gold, gypsum plaster, faience, glass, stone and glue. The two most important materials were wood and rawhide. For the basic chassis of the vehicle, as well as its axle, wheels, pole and yoke (and sometimes, as in the case of Tutankhamun, the blinkers), various different types of wood were required – particularly ash (*Fraxinus excelsior*), imported from outside Egypt, which was used for the axle, felloes and frame. Two other imported woods were also used: field maple (*Acer campestre*) was used for the floor of the Florence chariot, and silver birch bark (*Betula pendula*) was used to cover an axle of a Tutankhamun chariot and also the axles of the Florence example. The purpose of the birch bark was almost certainly to waterproof the glue and rawhide holding the chariot together; it seems to have been used in the same way to waterproof composite bows. Willow (*Salix subserrata*, which is found in Egypt) was used for the Florence chariot's pole, and elm (*Ulmus minor*, an import) was used for its yoke, handrail and wheel spindles. Elm was also used in the chariot from the tomb of Amenhotep III. Plum-wood (not found in Egypt) was sometimes used for the spokes, while locally available acacia was used for the front of the chassis.

The craftsmen would have needed to use a steam-bending technique to manufacture the chariot chassis and wheels, using strips of unseasoned timber. There are also scenes in the 5th-Dynasty tombs of Ptahshepses (at Abusir) and Ti (at Saqqara) showing the bending of dampened unseasoned poles of timber for unknown purposes. This type of technology had therefore clearly been available long before chariots began to be manufactured by Egyptians in the late 2nd millennium BC.

Leather was used for the many thongs and pieces of harness required for chariotry, but it was also used to extensively sheath any surfaces likely to suffer stress or abrasion. In addition, rawhide was shrunk over the composite wheels to hold them together and provide a form of tyre, and leather traces were used to lash the central pole to the yoke.

Textiles were used, primarily for 'kickboards', floor matting and housing.

Since the Egyptians already had access to nearly all of the specific materials and technology needed for chariot production by the Middle Kingdom, it is likely that the adoption of chariotry was primarily held up by social and political issues. It was probably not until the early New Kingdom that the development of a greater sphere of influence in the Near East gave them ready access to such imports as horses and exotic woods (ash, elm and birch). More importantly, perhaps, although they had most of the necessary *individual* skills and craftsmen to produce chariot components, they evidently did not acquire the collective methods and personnel to transform these discrete craftsmen into *teams* of chariot-builders until the early New Kingdom, when such craftsmen either arrived of their own volition or were among the prisoners of war brought back from early 18th-Dynasty military campaigns into the Levant. Once they were able to import materials, craftsmen, horses and experienced charioteers, they could begin to create their own vehicles and to incorporate chariotry and horse-riding 'scout' divisions into their own military strategies.

The second victory stele of King Kamose of the late 17th Dynasty (c.1550 BC) appears to contain the first Egyptian textual reference to a chariot, although the terminology used is quite different to that of New Kingdom texts, which, as noted above, usually employ the words *wrryt, mrkbt* or *ṯprṯ*. The first (and earliest) of these, *wrryt,* is used not only for chariots but also for other kinds of wheeled vehicles, such as ox- or donkey-carts. It has usually been assumed that *wrryt* was an Asiatic (or even Indo-European) loan-word, but no definite antecedents in such languages as Hurrian have actually been identified, so it is also possible that the word is simply a derivation of the Egyptian word *wr* ('great').

In contrast to *wrryt*, the term *mrkbt* is definitely an Asiatic loan-word (deriving from the city-state of Ugarit in Syria-Palestine), and seems to refer only to chariots. It appears for the first time in the Karnak stele of Amenhotep II (c.1427–1400 BC), when it is used to refer to the chariot of an Asiatic prince (perhaps deliberately in contrast to the text's reference to the Egyptian king's *wrryt*) and continued to be used to refer to chariots through to the Roman period. During the course of the New Kingdom, *mrkbt* gradually replaced *wrryt* as the main term for chariot. The use and meaning of the rare word *t̠prt̠*, which only appears twice in Egyptian texts, is slightly more disputed: it was once assumed to refer to a Hittite style of chariot (in contrast to the Egyptian type), but it is now thought to have been used to describe carts or wagons in the 19th–20th dynasties. It is unclear whether *t̠prt̠* is an indigenous Egyptian term or a loan-word (although it has been suggested that it might derive from the Akkadian *sappuru*: 'cart'). There is also an extensive range of terminology relating to individual chariot parts (such as 'pole' and 'floor'), many of which appear to be Asiatic loan-words.

The victory stele of Kamose uses the unusual phrase 'the one concerning the oxen/horses', which is usually taken to refer to chariots used by the Hyksos in their battles against Kamose. It is also notable that the stele seems to refer only to Hyksos chariots, implying that they were not yet being used by the Egyptian army in the late 17th Dynasty; however, texts in the Elkab tomb of Ahmose son of Ibana (a soldier who served in the armies of Ahmose, Amenhotep I and Thutmose I) include several references to chariots, suggesting that Egyptians had begun to use chariots no later than the reign of Ahmose, at the very beginning of the 18th Dynasty.

Where did the chariotry horses come from?

The earliest skeleton of a horse so far found in Egypt and Nubia is the carcass discovered at the Buhen fortress in Lower Nubia, dating to *c.*1680–1640 BC. The Buhen horse measured 125 centimetres high at the shoulders, slightly shorter than the average chariot horse, judging from the yoke measurements of surviving chariots. Another horse, with a shoulder height of about 142 cm, was buried in western Thebes (Luxor) beside one of the tombs of Senenmut (TT71), chief of works in the reign of Queen Hatshepsut. The Senenmut horse was mummified in linen bandages and placed in a 2.5-metre-long wooden coffin, whereas the Buhen example seems to have been encased in mud-brick walling built over the spot where it died. A third horse was found in the 18th-Dynasty necropolis at Soleb in

Nubia, and its height was between about 134 and 138cm at the shoulder. Three horses were also buried in a re-used tomb at Saqqara, but these can only be dated very vaguely to some point between the 20th Dynasty and the Ptolemaic period (*c.*1186–30 BC). Both the Buhen and Senenmut horses appear to be of the Arabian breed, suggesting that the earliest examples were probably imported or plundered from Western Asia. According to his *Annals* in the Temple of Amun at Karnak, the 18th-Dynasty ruler Thutmose III captured more than 2,000 horses after the battle of Megiddo, and the roughly contemporary Theban tomb of Amunedjeh actually includes painted wall decoration showing horses being brought by Syrians as tribute.

The first textual reference to horses in Egypt occurs in the late 17th-Dynasty victory stele of Kamose, which mentions those used by the Hyksos. That the term used for a span of horses, *ḥtri*, is an Asiatic loan-word suggests that both the animals and the techniques for training and utilizing them derived from Western Asia. It should be noted, however, that there are also strong connections between the Nubians and horses. Although the clearest evidence for Nubia as a widely recognized international source of horses and trainers begins with the 25th Dynasty, there are also earlier indications of Nubian horsemanship, therefore Nubia should not be ruled out as a possible source of horses even as early as the Second Intermediate Period, which is probably when the Buhen horse should be dated. It may be significant in this regard that two of our very small group of surviving early Egyptian horses were actually found in Nubia. This is particularly interesting when we bear in mind that the Thebans were evidently as much cut off from the Kerma culture in Nubia as they were from Syria-Palestine and the Mediterranean during the Second Intermediate Period.

Egyptian chariots appear to have differed from their Hittite and Syrian counterparts in a number of ways. Whereas the Hittite and Syrian chariots are shown with three occupants, comprising a shield-bearer in front of the driver and a spearman behind him, and apparently no quivers for arrows or javelins, the Egyptian chariots had a two-man crew and are shown with quivers attached for the archer.

CHAPTER 6

CULTURE, ETHNICITY, AND MOBILITY OF SOLDIERS AND WEAPONS

From at least the Early Dynastic Period onwards, the Egyptian army had frequently included foreign soldiers, and initially these seem to have been primarily Nubian (*nḥsyw*). Soldiers deriving from various Nubian ethnic groups are mentioned as serving in the Egyptian military by the late Old Kingdom and First Intermediate Period (c.2350–2050 BC); at this date the geographical location of Nubia is usually rendered as *tꜣ stỉ* or *nḥsỉ*. A tomb at Gebelein yielded the funerary stele of a man who is clearly identified as a Nubian soldier living and plying his trade in Egypt; his name, Ihetek, appears to have an etymology relating to the language of bedouin in the southern part of the Eastern Desert. At the tomb of Setka in Aswan there is a late Old Kingdom (or perhaps First Intermediate Period) scene of several Nubian archers (see Chapter 1). Probably these Nubians at Gebelein and Aswan were a mixture of C-Group and Medjay ethnic groups, with perhaps even a few from the emerging kingdom of Kerma, that would eventually gain control of Nubia during the Second Intermediate Period.

The Medjay, a semi-nomadic, cattle-herding group originally from the eastern desert of Nubia, were commonly employed as scouts and light infantry in the Egyptian army from the Second Intermediate Period onwards. Papyrus Boulaq 18, an early 13th-Dynasty set of royal court records, includes a description of the arrival of a delegation of eight Medjay and also the appearance of a Medjay prince. One of the Semna Despatches describes the arrival of a group of starving Medjay wishing to enlist with the Egyptian army, while another describes the apprehending and interrogation of a group of Medjay. The victory stele of the late 17th-Dynasty ruler Kamose mentions the use of Medjay troops by Kamose in his campaign against the Hyksos, who controlled northern Egypt during the Second Intermediate Period (*c.*1650–1550 BC).

The Medjay – purely attested by texts and visual images – have often been identified with the archaeological remains of the so-called Pan-grave people, a group initially pursuing a semi-nomadic existence in the eastern deserts of Egypt and Nubia who eventually, like the Medjay, appear to have been absorbed into the mainstream Egyptian population. Although the link between Medjay and Pan-grave culture is plausible, it remains a hypothesis. The characteristic feature of the Pan-grave culture is the shallow circular pit-grave in which they buried their dead, examples of which are known throughout Upper Egypt and Lower Nubia. The graves preserve the typically Nubian tradition of burying skulls and horns of gazelles, oxen and sheep, sometimes painted. An ox-skull from grave 3252 in a Pan-grave cemetery at Mostagedda in Upper Egypt (British Museum EA63339) is painted with a human image that appears to

Scene of five Nubian Medjay mercenaries from the tomb of the 'commander of soldiers', Tjanuny, at Thebes (TT74), New Kingdom, c.1410 BC; the soldier on the right carries a military standard bearing a depiction of wrestlers.

portray a nomadic chieftain with his weapons (axe, club and shield); the man's name, Qeskanet, is written in hieroglyphs, showing that contact between the Pan-grave group and the Egyptian population was well established.

By the 18th Dynasty, soldiers of many different ethnicities had begun to be drafted into the Egyptian ranks, often in the form of branded prisoners permitted to win their freedom by taking up arms on behalf of Egypt. Some foreign soldiers were clearly able to be well integrated into Egyptian society. A painted limestone stele excavated from a house in the late 18th-Dynasty city at Amarna (Berlin, Ägyptisches Museum) shows a Syrian mercenary in an elaborate kilt apparently relaxing with his wife, while an Egyptian servant helps him drink from a pottery jar through a Near Eastern type of reed straw.

In the late New Kingdom, Egypt came into conflict with a wide diversity of ethnic groups in Syria-Palestine, in the eastern Mediterranean, and in the area to the northwest of Egypt (now occupied by modern Libya). They frequently took large numbers

Painted limestone stele from Amarna (Ägyptisches Museum Berlin 14122), showing a Syrian mercenary named Terer (Dalilu?) drinking beer or wine with his wife, Irbura, and a servant, while his spear is leaning against the wall behind him, c.1350 BC.

of prisoners of war, many of whom were then absorbed into the ranks of the army as 'mercenary' troops. It is also possible that some of these foreign troops voluntarily chose to become part of the Egyptian army. Among such foreign mercenaries were the Meshwesh and Libu, who were often shown with feathers on their heads and armed with bows. Perhaps the most distinctive – in terms of arm and armour – were the Sherden, one of the groups described as Sea Peoples (see Chapter 8). The origins of the Sherden perhaps lay in northern Syria but, as far as the Egyptian records are concerned they first appeared as part of Ramesses II's army in his campaigns against the Hittites. The Sherden typically fought with sword and spear, and they are instantly recognizable by their unusual headgear, a round leather helmet (sometimes with cheek protectors) surmounted by a pair of curving horns on either side of a spike, which is itself sometimes topped by a sphere or disc. They also carry a round shield and wear a distinctive kilt, longer at the back than the front. The long tapering sword with which they are often armed is not specific to the Sherden but a lengthened form of a common type of dagger used throughout the Levant during the Middle Bronze Age.

In one of Ramesses II's earlier campaigns in Syria-Palestine a group of foreign mercenaries, wearing tasselled kilts and carrying round shields decorated with bosses, are shown storming the fortress

A group of Sherden mercenary soldiers depicted on the external wall of the Temple of Ramesses II at Abydos, c.1250 BC.

of Deper in Amurru – their horned helmets (unusually shown in profile) suggest that they may have been Sherden, although no spike or disc is shown in the centre of the helmet. In Merneptah's first war against the 'Libyans' (i.e. Meshwesh and Libu) towards the end of 13th century BC, the Sherden appear as allies of the Libyans, fighting against the Egyptians, although they appear to be distinguishable from the Egyptianized Sherden by their helmets, which firstly were shaped to the backs of their necks and secondly, as with the unnamed mercenaries at Deper, had no disc-shape between the horns.

Movement of people and weapons

If Late Bronze Age military tactics can be argued to be relatively homogeneous throughout Egypt and the rest of the Near East during the Bronze Age, and perhaps only significantly influenced by differences in terrain, topography and overall political aims, what is the situation concerning soldiers and weaponry? How much overlap was there between the characteristics of the troops and weaponry used by Hittites and Egyptians, for example? Whereas the Hittites own depictions portray their soldiers as wearing short belted tunics only reaching down to a point above the knee, the Egyptian reliefs suggest that Hittite soldiers wore long gowns with short sleeves.

The ways in which weapon types are portrayed can also differ between cultures: the figure of a Hittite warrior-god from the jamb of the King's Gate at Hattusa (Boghazköy) is depicted wearing a belted kilt and helmet, and is armed with an axe and short sword, whereas the typical Egyptian image of the Hittite soldier tends to show him carrying a spear, which is usually not portrayed by the Hittite artists until a later date. One possible answer to these discrepancies is that many of the soldiers depicted in the Egyptian reliefs were not actually Hittites, but other ethnic types from within the Hittite empire. Another likely answer, however, is an artistic one – perhaps the Egyptians deliberately depict the Hittites and their allies in this non-Egyptian costume to clearly distinguish them from the Egyptian soldiers, whose short kilt would otherwise have easily been confused with that of the enemy.

Some of the detailed images of the Egyptian ruler Akhenaten's first campaign against the Hittites show the enemy with pigtail-style

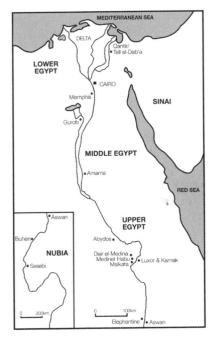

sidelocks. The Hittites are also shown wearing a distinctive squat, open-faced helmet with a neck protector and plumed crest (the so-called 'plumed bronze helmet' typically found in the Near East in the late 2nd millennium BC), which is the kind of headgear worn by the warrior god at Boghazköy. Akhenaten's artists, however, show this helmet being worn by both Hittites and Egyptians, suggesting further blurring of the traditionally strict boundaries of weaponry and costume.

Map of Egypt showing major New Kingdom cities, including Amarna, Memphis, Thebes (Luxor) and Piramesse (Qantir). (Paul Vyse)

In the 1983–84 seasons of excavation at Qantir (the site of the Ramesside city of Piramesse), in the Egyptian eastern Delta, eight limestone 'moulds' for shields were found, each measuring around 1.25 × 1.25 metres. Remarkably, these moulds were clearly not designed to produce the standard Egyptian rectangular shield; instead they were intended to produce typical Hittite trapezoidal or 'figure-of-eight' shields, one incorporating a stylized version of a bull's head probably referring to a Hittite weather-god. The craftsmen at Piramesse would have used the moulds to hammer out sheets of copper alloy forming the outer edges of the wood and leather shields. This seems to be evidence of direct collaboration between Egyptian and Hittite workers, operating on Egyptian soil, to produce weaponry that would usually be regarded as fundamentally non-Egyptian. The excavator, Edgar Pusch, argues that the dating of the Hittite shield moulds could theoretically relate to one or other of three events in the reign of Ramesses II: the arrival in Egypt of the deposed Hittite ruler Urhi Teshup; the year 21 peace-treaty between

Ramesses and the Hittite ruler Hattusilis III, and the year 34 marriage to the Hittite princess who was given the Egyptian name of Maat-hor-neferu-ra, recorded in the 'marriage stele' at Abu Simbel. He suggests that the last of these is most likely, on the grounds of the stratigraphic position of one of the shield-moulds (linking it with pillars inscribed with the texts dating to Ramesses II's 30th regnal year).

The scenario for this Egypto-Hittite technological exchange must belong to the Ramesside period, when cities like Piramesse included many foreigners within their populations, some of whom eventually became high-ranking officials within the Egyptian administration. Additionally, as a result of at least two peace treaties between Egypt and the Hittites, specialist craftsmen were evidently sent by Egypt's former enemy to work in military workshops, such as those at Piramesse, passing on to the Egyptians the technology to produce non-Egyptian styles of weaponry, including the Hittite shields for which moulds were found.

The spread of military wares

What were the practical mechanisms by which military tactics and weaponry spread across northeast Africa, the East Mediterranean and the Near East in the Late Bronze Age? 'Mercenary' soldiers, such as the Sherden, seem to have brought with them their own types of weaponry and presumably also different methods of fighting. This seems to have happened both with 'free' mercenaries and with enforced prisoner-of-war-style mercenaries. Diplomacy (through exchange of people and artefacts and through establishment of 'embassies') was probably the other principal mechanism by which people, things and ideas moved across state boundaries.

The coincidence of several features of recent excavations at Qantir (Piramesse), suggests that diplomatic activity and technology transfer might have been closely linked. Not only have the Hittite shield moulds, described above, been found, but in 1999, in the area of the city designated QVII, part of a cuneiform tablet was unearthed, raising the possibility that a Ramesside international diplomatic archive (like the well-known late 18th-Dynasty one at Amarna; see Chapter 8) might have existed in the vicinity. Even if this small fragment – only 5 × 5 cm and bearing just 11 lines of text – turns out to be an isolated find, it hints at the possibility that the population of Piramesse included not only Hittite craftsmen but also perhaps a relatively permanent staff of Hittite 'embassy' officials. The finds of shield-moulds and tablet are linked by letter EA22, a tablet in the Amarna archive that was sent by Tushratta, ruler of the Western Asiatic kingdom of Mitanni to Amenhotep III of Egypt, in which a list of elite diplomatic gifts sent to Egypt includes 'one leather shield with *urukmannu* of silver weighing ten shekels' (the Hurrian term *urukmannu* probably referring to the outer metal parts of a shield, for which the Qantir moulds would have been used).

The excavations at Qantir have also yielded a worked boar's tusk that may have been part of a cheek-piece from a Mycenaean-style helmet. Once again a find from Amarna provides a context both confirming the integration of 'foreign' equipment within Egyptian weaponry and the likely long-term nature of such integration and exchange: fragments of a painted papyrus (British Museum, EA74100) excavated from building R43.2 in the late 18th-Dynasty central city at Amarna include two soldiers within the Egyptian army apparently depicted wearing boar's tusk helmets and cropped ox-hide tunics, which would probably identify them as Mycenaean infantry within the Egyptian army in the mid-14th century BC. The presence of a fragment of such a helmet at Qantir suggests that other non-Egyptian weaponry may have been used, and perhaps even manufactured, at the city of Piramesse in the Ramesside period. The Qantir and Amarna finds paint a possible picture of Near Eastern movements of soldiers and transfer of military technology taking place within a diplomatic context for much of the New Kingdom.

Fragment of a cuneiform tablet, excavated from the city of Piramesse (Qantir), l. 5cm, w. 5cm, c.1250 BC. (Axel Krause, courtesy of the Qantir-Pi-Ramesse Project)

Military strategies and policies in the Near East during the Late Bronze Age

How did the Late Bronze Age 'Great Powers', such as the Egyptians, Mitannians, Hittites and Assyrians, differ from one another in terms of their specific military strategies? With regard to the broadest strategic and political sphere of warfare, a fair amount of evidence has survived for Hittite and Egyptian responses to the ideas of empire-building and conquest. Interestingly, one similarity between the Egyptian and Hittite empires' military strategy is their tendency to maintain a pretence that kings did not aggressively instigate wars, but simply responded to events. Even at the height of the Hittite empire, its rulers and their officials might be considered to have been in a state of denial as to their repeated undertaking of hostile acts of conquest. The same situation has also been argued to prevail in Egypt, where the pharaoh is frequently portrayed as a passive component, only reacting after he has been informed of foreign unrest. In both cases, these were probably calculated postures deliberately evoked by both the Egyptian and Hittite texts, while the real situation can sometimes be read, between the lines, as one of ruthless pragmatism. Nevertheless, the fact remains that two of the major powers of the Late Bronze Age east Mediterranean share a tendency to consciously and purposefully present foreign conquests almost as accidents rather than as the result of careful hardheaded strategies, whereas the latter is the clear impression given by Late Bronze Age diplomatic correspondence between the Egyptian rulers and their rivals and vassals in Western Asia.

It tends to be automatically assumed that Egyptian battles were opportunist, unpredictable affairs, but we know some Classical Greek conflicts involved an element of ritual, not merely in the way that battles were depicted but in terms of actual confrontations between armies. Some scholars have argued that the locations and dates of the Megiddo and Qadesh battles (the details of which are discussed in Chapter 4) might have been pre-arranged by the two sides. Most researchers would probably not agree with so radical an interpretation of the surviving reliefs and papyri documenting these two events, which seem too unique and idiosyncratic to be regarded as mere large-scale ritualistic encounters. However, there are certain recurring motifs (such as the king's heroism in adversity and the tendency for texts to portray him as suggesting risky tactics in place of the cautious plans of generals) that imply that the accounts of the battles are at least as much literary as historical. The ways in which these conflicts are said to take place suggest a high degree of spontaneity, and it seems unlikely that there was anything as predictable as the clash of hoplite phalanxes in Greek battles of the 8th–7th centuries BC. Thus, although the time and place of crucial battles in the Late Bronze Age may at least sometimes have been pre-arranged, their actual details were usually unpredictable.

In *The Instruction Addressed to King Merikara*, the alleged author (named as Khety, an Egyptian ruler of the Herakleopolitan period, *c.*2160–2025 BC) complains that 'the vile Asiatic…does not announce the day of battle, like a thief whom a gang has rejected…The Asiatic is a crocodile on its river bank that snatches from a lonely road but cannot take from the quay of a populous town'. Although Asiatic armies often appear to be criticized, in Egyptian texts, for their apparent use of guerilla tactics, it may nevertheless be the case that the Egyptians used such methods themselves. At Qadesh and in the campaigns against the Sea Peoples, for instance, there are indications of the use of surprise tactics. In the various depictions of the battle of Qadesh, Ramesses required several forms of last-minute assistance from his own troops to allow him defeat the vast number of enemies pitted against him. In three instances he is helped by charioteers, who, in one case, trap the Hittites occupying the area behind the king, in what appears to be one of the earliest records of an ambush. Both Papyrus Harris I and the inscriptions at Medinet Habu, recording Ramesses III's sea and land battles against the Sea Peoples, suggest that the victories each involved an ambush, or a surprise attack of combined Egyptian military units on a cornered mass of Sea Peoples.

The lingua franca of Bronze Age warfare

This chapter has suggested that the panoramic New Kingdom temple reliefs depicting battles have a tendency to oversimplify the situation – the Egyptian depictions sometimes accentuate the ethnic stereotypes of individual soldiers, and to make the battles easier to 'read' as narratives of confrontations between state armies, they use a kind of visual shorthand with which we need to deal very cautiously. This shorthand draws on longstanding iconography concerning the typical characteristics of foreigners, which is exemplified very effectively by the images of a Nubian and an Asiatic at either end of the handle of a walking cane from the tomb of Tutankhamun. However, if some of the ethnic and cultural details of these battle reliefs are interpreted sufficiently carefully – and placed in the context of the recent finds, such as the Hittite material at Qantir – we can gain a strong sense of the complex reservoir of weaponry and tactics from which each of the great states of the Late Bronze Age East Mediterranean were drawing. In other words, the features that appear to be typically Hittite, Syrian, Cretan, Mycenaean or Egyptian about armies, and in particular their weaponry and tactics, need to be balanced against the *lingua franca* of warfare that undoubtedly existed. None of these armies existed in isolation from one another, and although there clearly were differences between the major armies at each point in time, such as the different style and manning of Hittite chariots compared with those of the Egyptians at Qadesh, they also had a great deal in common, and the degree to which they shared tactics, weaponry and personnel is not to be underestimated.

Soldiers, tactics and weaponry evidently ebbed and flowed between different armies and states rather than being fixed components of ethnic groups. This also has repercussions for our approach to the study of ancient weaponry, the technology and dissemination of which may not have been so clearly delineated by cultural and ethnic boundaries as previous assumed. Egyptian military technology may have existed and evolved within a particularly rich context of cultural exchange networks, which we are arguably underestimating by our tendency to stereotype them in ethnic terms.

CHAPTER 7

————•— ———•— ———•— ———•—

NAVAL BATTLES

A GREAT DEAL OF INFORMATION HAS survived concerning Egyptian ships and boats, principally in the form of depictions on the walls of tombs, funerary models and textual references. There have also been a number of finds of actual boats, ranging from the reconstructed solar bark of Khufu (*c*.2589–2566 BC) to the fragments of boat timber preserved through their reuse for such purposes as the construction of slipways. The prevailing wind in the Nile Valley came from the north, so that sails could be used to propel boats travelling south, while those heading north, against the wind, relied on oars and the current. For this reason, the hieroglyph for 'travelling north', even in the case of overland travel, consisted of a boat with its sails down, while that for 'travelling south' shows a boat with billowing sails.

Probably the earliest and simplest boats were papyrus skiffs, made of bundles of reeds lashed together. These would have been used for fishing and hunting game in the marshes, for crossing the river, and for travelling short distances, and this type probably remained in use for some purposes throughout pharaonic history. Even from Predynastic times there is evidence for larger vessels, though perhaps still of reed construction. Boats were commonly depicted in red paint on some of the buff-coloured pottery of the Naqada II (or Gerzean) period (*c*.3500–3200 BC). These images include some showing elaborate, many-oared, ships crewed by numerous sailors. The prows and sterns of such vessels are usually upturned; they would normally have been provided with at least one large steering oar, and sometimes also a sail and cabin. This late Predynastic imagery also includes boats with high, straight prows and sterns,

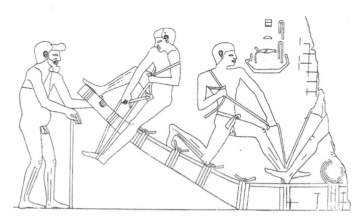

Scene of papyrus gathering and, at the right hand side, construction of a papyrus skiff, from the Middle Kingdom tomb of Ukhhotep II, son of Senbi, at Meir, c.1940 BC. (line drawing: Paul Vyse; after A. W. Blackman, The Rock Tombs of Meir II (London, 1915): pls 3–4)

sometimes interpreted as foreign vessels, although there is no real evidence to support this view.

The Gebel el-Arak knife-handle

Elaborately carved ceremonial knives with ivory handles, dating between the Naqada IId period and the 1st Dynasty (i.e. *c.*3300–3000 BC), constitute a significant source on late Predynastic culture, as discussed in Chapter 1 (along with the roughly contemporary ceremonial palettes and mace-heads). The carved relief decoration on one particular Naqada II ivory knife-handle, allegedly from Gebel el-Arak and now in the Louvre, is a set of images that some researchers have interpreted as the earliest Egyptian depiction of a sea or river battle. These 'naval' images appear to comprise depictions of two different types of boat: the familiar crescent-shaped Egyptian papyrus skiff and another type with an almost vertical prow. Between the two rows of boats, two sets of sprawling human bodies are represented – these are usually interpreted either as captives, or, more likely, slaughtered enemies, thus implying that the boats were engaged in some kind of violent action.

Shortly after the knife-handle's publication, Flinders Petrie argued that it was part of the evidence for the conquest of Egypt by the so-called 'dynastic race' at the beginning of Egyptian history. Petrie's 'dynastic race' theory for the origins of Egyptian civilization has long since been rejected (and replaced by more complex ideas concerning the emergence and codification of a standardized indigenous Egyptian culture during the late 4th millennium BC) but there are still scholars who would argue that that the decoration on the knife-handle may record a military encounter between Egyptians and foreign (perhaps Near Eastern or Libyan) invaders. However, two points might be made here. Firstly, even if this is a rendition of conflict between different types of boats, it may simply represent generic motifs of violence and power rather than portraying a specific military event. Secondly, our knowledge of early boat types in north Africa and the Near East is not sufficiently detailed to allow us to say that this battle is between two groups with radically different ethnic, cultural or geographical origins.

Old and Middle Kingdom boats

By the Old Kingdom, there are sufficient surviving images, models and surviving examples of boats to allow us to build up a general idea of their types and uses. The boats and ships of the Old Kingdom were usually made of wood obtained either locally or from Syria-Palestine. They had a characteristically curving hull and were provided with several steering oars, a mast, and a long narrow sail. Oars would also have been used for propulsion when there was insufficient breeze to fill the sails. The best-known surviving Old Kingdom boat is that excavated from a pit beside the pyramid of Khufu at Giza, which was 43.6 metres long and made of large planks of cedar wood, 'sewn' together with ropes. It had a deck but no keel, and was furnished with twelve oars for its propulsion. This was a 'solar barge', probably intended to function ceremonially and/or as part of the king's afterlife, rather than being a vessel that was actually used for practical purposes (although it has been argued that it might have been used to transport the king's body to the pyramid): Nevertheless, it still gives us a very good idea of materials and construction techniques.

Boatbuilding was a craft with a long tradition in Egypt, as evidenced by the skilful craftsmanship used for Khufu's boat. Textual records also suggest that boats were being constructed on a significant scale at an even earlier date – thus, the Palermo Stone (a 5th-Dynasty 'king-list') records the construction of a ship 52 metres (170 feet) in length during the reign of Sneferu (c.2613–2589 BC), Khufu's immediate predecessor. In the 5th-Dynasty tomb of Ti (c.2450 BC) at Saqqara, boatbuilders are depicted at work on various stages of the construction of a large wooden vessel. River-going barges appear to have been used to transport stone from the quarries to the construction sites of pyramid complexes – thus the reliefs decorating the causeway of the late 5th-Dyasty pyramid complex of Unas (c.2375–2345 BC) included depictions of the boats carrying the huge granite papyrus columns for his valley temple.

From around the 6th Dynasty onwards, the steering oar was operated as a rudder by means of ropes, but in most other respects the typical craft of the Middle Kingdom were similar in design to those of the Old Kingdom. The mast on many Middle Kingdom boats seems to have been collapsible, and rested on a stand when not in use, while the cabin was usually located at the stern. Many models of these boats have survived in tombs, where they played an important role in the funerary cult, symbolizing the journey of the deceased to Abydos. There are also surviving fragments of timber from actual vessels reused for slipways and ramps in the Middle Kingdom pyramid complexes at Lisht. A set of well-preserved dismantled wooden boats were found by excavators at Mersa Gawasis on the Red Sea coast in 2005.

So what evidence do we have for the military use of boats at this date? In the Old and Middle kingdoms, Nile boats seem to have been sometimes used for the transportation of troops up and down the Nile. In addition, the reliefs in the 5th-Dynasty mortuary temple of King Sahura (c.2487–2475 BC) at Abusir depict a sea-borne fleet that is said to have transported his army to Syria. In the 6th Dynasty, the official Weni is said to have taken troops to a location named as 'Nose of Gazelle's Head', usually thought to be in southern Palestine, using vessels described as *nmiw* ('travelling-ships').

Most Egyptian boats, however, were unsuitable for sailing in the Mediterranean or the Red Sea. The impetus for seaborne trade, therefore, seems to have come from the Levantine seaboard, probably

Boatbuilders shown constructing a large wooden vessel, in the 5th-Dynasty tomb of Ti (c.2450 BC) at Saqqara.

in the region of Byblos. Certainly there was a strong connection in Egyptian minds between Byblos and naval activity, since the most common word for an Egyptian sea-going vessel was *kbnt*, literally 'Byblos-boat'. It is not clear, however, whether the use of the term denotes Byblos' importance as a centre for boatbuilding, its role as a source of timber or its familiarity as a regular destination of merchant vessels – all three explanations are equally likely. The first references to a 'Byblos-boat' occur in a 5th-Dynasty inscription at Ayn Sukhna and a 6th-Dynasty text in the tomb of Pepynakht at Aswan. Pepynakht describes an expedition to recover the body of a murdered Egyptian who had been sent to Western Asia (or perhaps the Red Sea coast of southern Sinai) to oversee the construction of a Byblos-boat intended for use on an expedition through the Red Sea to the land of Punt (probably located in southern Sudan and/ or Somalia). This text therefore suggests that, in the Old Kingdom at least, Egyptians may have depended at least in part on Asiatic boat-builders for their sea-going ships.

New Kingdom boats

In the New Kingdom, vessels seem to have become more specialized; there were usually cabins on both the stern and the prow, in addition to a main cabin in the centre of the boat. The helmsman operated double steering oars by a system of ropes and levers as before, and the width of the sail was greater than its height. As in the Old Kingdom, huge masses of stone were also moved by barge, including obelisks for the temple of Hatshepsut (*c.*1473–1458 BC) at Deir el-Bahari. The same queen also sent a sea-borne trading expedition to the kingdom of Punt (probably located in modern South Sudan or Eritrea). The Egyptian navy of the late New Kingdom was put to the test when it repulsed invasions of so-called Sea Peoples, with a significant naval battle in the reign of Rameses III (*c.*1184–1153 BC) being recorded both visually and textually in some detail (see below). A late 20th-Dynasty literary (or possibly quasi-historical) text, *The Report of Wenamun*, outlines a difficult and eventful sea-journey by the eponymous official Wenamun, to obtain timber from Byblos.

Even the sea-going boats used by the New Kingdom Egyptians and their neighbours were relatively simple, consisting of a rectangular sail and one or two rudder oars. When there was no following wind, tacking was not possible, and the boats had to be propelled by rowers. However, the Bronze Age wrecks excavated at Cape Gelidonya and Ulu Burun (both sites in the eastern Mediterranean) indicate the crucial role played by small wooden cargo ships in the flow of goods across the Mediterranean between southern Europe and the Near East. It has been estimated that the Levantine port of Ugarit had as many as 150 boats in its navy, and one of the Amarna Letters records a request for the King of Alashiya (almost certainly Cyprus) to build ships for the Egyptian navy. This is one of the early indications of increasing links between the Egyptians and the Greeks, in terms of the exploitation and control of the Mediterranean.

The 'Sea Peoples'

For most of the dynastic period, activities on the Mediterranean sea appear to have mainly been characterized by commerce rather than military aggression (although hard evidence of any kind relating to naval activity prior to the late 1st millennium BC is hard to find). In the late New Kingdom, however, visual and textual sources suggest that a number of sea-borne foreign armies began to menace the Delta coastline, posing a new kind of challenge to the pharaohs. On an international level, various natural and political disasters along the northern coast of the Mediterranean appear to have precipitated widespread migrations and invasions that plunged the Mediterranean region into a period of conflict and instability.

In the second year of the reign of Ramesses II (*c.*1278 BC) there was a raid by Sherden pirates, who were defeated and incorporated into the Egyptian army as an elite force of mercenaries. This was the first indication, from Egyptian sources, that a real threat was posed by a loose confederation of sea-going Indo-European migrants – including the Ekwesh, Shekelesh, Tjeker, Weshesh, Teresh, Sherden, Lukka and Denyen – whom the Egyptians described as the 'Sea Peoples' or simply as 'northerners'. It was perhaps partly as an attempt to prevent further incursions by the Sea Peoples that Ramesses II built a row of fortresses along the northwestern coastline of Egypt (although see Chapter 2 for fuller discussion of their likely role).

In the fifth year of Merenptah's reign (*c.*1207 BC) an alliance of Tjehenu, Meshwesh and Sea Peoples attempted to invade Egypt, again from the northwest. These armies had brought with them their families and possessions, suggesting that their intention was to settle rather than simply to plunder. The battle with which Merenptah eventually repelled this first wave of Sea Peoples is recorded on a wall of the temple at Karnak. The inscriptions record that 6,000 Sea Peoples were killed and 9,000 taken prisoner, but numbers in texts of this genre can obviously not be taken at face value. It is probably no coincidence that the same inscription records the sending of grain to the ailing Hittite empire of Tudhaliyas IV – the attacks of the Sea Peoples from the north were evidently setting off a chain reaction of invasions and population movements along the entire Levantine seaboard, including the areas controlled by the Hittites. Neither Egypt nor the cities of Syria-Palestine could afford to allow the Hittite empire to fall into decline, since this would eventually leave a dangerous power vacuum, allowing the Sea Peoples to sweep down through Anatolia.

The Medinet Habu reliefs

Over thirty years later, in the eighth year of the reign of Ramesses III (*c.*1174 BC), a second wave of Sea Peoples arrived on the Delta border. On this occasion they were allied with the Peleset (Philistines) and their attack came from the northeast by both land and sea. One of the inscriptions in the temple at Medinet Habu – the main source for Ramesses III's battle with the Sea

Peoples – describes their advance: 'Suddenly these peoples were on the move, scattered in war. No country could withstand their arms. The Hittites, Cilicia, Carcemish, Cyprus and other lands were cut off'. The same source tells us that the Sea Peoples' land attack was checked by a single battle in the region of the Egyptian frontier garrisons along the northern edge of the Sinai desert. In the description of this land conflict it is noticeable that, as in the reign of Merenptah, the invaders are described as being accompanied by their families, ox-carts and livestock.

When the Sea Peoples transferred their energies to an attack by sea, Ramesses III defeated them again in a great naval battle, which was depicted in a complex relief sculpture on the northern outer wall of his mortuary temple at Medinet Habu. These reliefs include depictions of ships that appear very similar, regardless of the occupants – all of them appear to be modified versions of Aegean light galleys and Late Bronze Age Syrian merchant ships (the latter being the prototype of the Phoenician *hippos* vessel). The relief shows hand-to-hand fighting between five of the Sea Peoples' boats (with prows and sterns carved in the form of birds' heads) and four of the larger Egyptian vessels (each with a lion's head at the prow). The Egyptian boats have rows of 20–22 oarsmen on board in addition to the archers and footsoldiers, whereas the smaller number of men on board the Sea Peoples' smaller boats must have doubled up as both warriors and rowers. One of the invaders' boats has been capsized, and the surrounding water is seething with dead Sea Peoples. Although the boats manned by Egyptian soldiers or their allies incorporate Egyptian-style hulls, the basic nature of each of them, in terms of such features as brailed rigging, crow's nest, platforms and overall 'fighting tops', is very similar, suggesting that the emerging sea-powers of the Late Bronze Age were not necessarily employing hardware that was culturally or ethnically distinct. It should be noted, however, that inscriptions accompanying the images of the naval battle mention three different types of vessel on the Egyptian side, despite the pictures only showing one form. One more cultural (rather than technological) way in which the portrayals of Sea Peoples' boats differed from those of the Egyptians was through the carving of both bow and stern to resemble birds' heads – this was typical Aegean marine iconography, judging from images of boats roughly contemporary with the Medinet Habu reliefs, e.g. the portrayal of a boat on a Late Helladic IIIc *krater* from Tiryns.

The boats of Sea Peoples and Egyptians, as depicted at Medinet Habu, both appear to have been very similar amalgams of East Mediterranean naval technology, and it is very tempting to assume that the type of boat the Egyptian artists portray as the characteristic vessels in the Egyptian navy at this date may actually have been introduced to Egypt by the Sea Peoples themselves. It is therefore possible that the particular specializations and technical innovations visible in both fleets depicted at Medinet Habu were the result of decades of previous naval encounters between the Sea Peoples, the Canaanites and the Egyptians. The development of the naval technology of the eastern Mediterranean in the Late Bronze Age seems to have involved extensive technology transfer even between supposed rivals. This may also have extended to tactics, with Ramesses III's army and navy evidently trapping the Sea Peoples by blockading the mouths of rivers, thereby 'catching the enemy like birds in a net' – this strategy may resemble 'riverine' tactics that were ascribed to the Sea Peoples themselves in a text from Ugarit. In Chapter 5 above, we examined the principal innovations in military technology that emerged in the Egyptian battles of the New Kingdom, and in particular the importance of the chariot's mobility. The Medinet Habu reliefs show that the same situation applied even to sea battles – thus, boats were used as sea-borne chariots containing groups of oarsmen, archers and footsoldiers. They allowed the Egyptians to encircle the enemy, while releasing hails of arrows, eventually closing in on the enemy's own boats, so that the infantry could engage in conventional hand-to-hand fighting.

So how are we to interpret the depictions of this battle on the exterior of the north wall of Medinet Habu? It presumably took place at some point in the Delta, probably along one of the Nile branches, rather than in the Mediterranean itself – one of the Medinet Habu inscriptions mentions that the Sea Peoples 'penetrated the channels of the river mouths'. One scholar (Harold Nelson) has argued that three groups of pairs of ships may represent

Egyptian boat in the naval battle portrayed on the external northern wall of the mortuary temple of Ramesses III, Medinet Habu, c.1170 BC.

three different temporal phases of the encounter, with a final, fourth phase being represented by a single Egyptian ship taking captives towards the shore. According to Nelson, a further pair of Sea Peoples' ships may be a naval version of the trope of defeated soldiers fleeing from the battle-place, which is a typical element in Ramesside portrayals of land battles.

The outcome of this naval encounter – the first sea battle to be documented and illustrated in detail – appears to have been another victory for Ramesses III. But, just as the Sherden had been assimilated into the Egyptian army after their defeat by Ramesses II, so the Sea Peoples were subsequently absorbed into the rapidly declining Egyptian empire. Although Ramesses III and his immediate successors still maintained control of Canaan, the Sea Peoples (particularly Peleset and Tjeker) were allowed to settle there.

This policy on the Sea Peoples must have been successful in the short term judging from an account of a Libyan attack in the eleventh year of Ramesses III's reign (*c.*1171 BC) in which the Sea Peoples are evidently no longer present as allies fighting against Egypt. But in the long term the Egyptians' solitary sea victory was only a postponement of the inevitable, and by the end of the 20th Dynasty, Canaan had effectively passed into the hands of the Sea Peoples. It is clear from the account of the ill-fated royal trading

Sea Peoples' boat in the naval battle portrayed on the external northern wall of the mortuary temple of Ramesses III, Medinet Habu, c.1170 BC.

mission of Wenamun (mentioned above) that, by the time of Ramesses XI and the priest-king Herihor (*c.*1075 BC), the Egyptian navy was unable even to maintain regular supplies of cedarwood from Byblos. The account of Wenamun's voyage mentions one stop-over at the port of Dor, which is specifically identified as being occupied by Tjeker people.

The Gurob boat One remarkable three-dimensional model of a Ramesside Egyptian boat points to significant cross-over between Egyptian and Aegean styles of sea-going boat in the New Kingdom. This painted wooden ritual artefact was discovered by Guy Brunton and Reginald Engelbach in 1920, in a late New Kingdom grave (Tomb 611) at Gurob. The artefact appears to represent a three-dimensional model of an Egyptian boat of this date, supported by a wheeled device. The design and construction of the boat has been clearly argued by Shelley Wachsman to be based on the prototype of the kind of galley used by Mycenaean sailors, and also by the Sea Peoples, even down to the stem-post terminating in a bird's head.

The boat model (radiocarbon-dated to around 1256–1054 BC) is most closely comparable, iconographically, to representations of

Mycenaean galleys of the Late Helladic IIIB-C period. However, as Wachsman points out, the rendering of the forecastle deck is very similar to models of Egyptian boats found in New Kingdom royal tombs, and the 'rockered' hull form is also said to be characteristically Egyptian. The boat's stanchions, on the other hand, which supported the superstructure and centre-line deck, seem to be one of the most distinctive and unique features of the Helladic galley, which was the prototype for subsequent forms of warship developed by both Greeks and Phoenicians.

Egyptian triremes: ramming war-galleys

The Egyptian warships used in the Late Period (*c*.664–332 BC) are often called triremes, and, as ramming war-galleys propelled by three superimposed banks of oars, they do seem to fit this definition. Opinions differ as to whether the trireme was first developed by Greeks or Phoenicians, but it is clear that, from *c*.700 BC onwards, both Phoenicians and Greeks were using two-decker warships created specifically for ramming, a tactic that became fairly standard across east Mediterranean cultures over subsequent centuries. The design of the Egyptian ships of the New Kingdom, however, would have been quite unsuitable for ramming, both because of the lack of a keel and the characteristic forward overhang at the prow. By the Late Period, it would therefore have become essential for Egyptians to acquire some form of trireme to allow them to compete with other naval powers.

Because the 26th-Dynasty Egyptian rulers appear to have initially come into conflict more with the Phoenicians than Greeks, they probably began to acquire triremes and crews from the latter, and then eventually gained the new boat-building, rowing and navigational skills to produce and sail their own. Furthermore, it would have been reasonably straightforward for such skills to have been acquired from Naukratis, a Greek trading colony situated within the Egyptian Delta and only ten miles from Sais, the 26th-Dynasty capital city. Late Period texts that mention the Egyptian fleet tend to refer to the ships with the term mentioned above: *kbnt*-boats (or 'Byblos-boats'). It is clear both from the contexts in which the term appears, and also from the changed appearance of the ideogram at the end of the word (the so-called determinative sign) that the word had by then come to mean not merely 'sea-going vessels' (as in the New Kingdom) but war-galleys built specifically for ramming.

Two 29th-Dynasty Egyptian rulers are documented as having sent large numbers of triremes to assist Greek allies: in 396 BC, the Egyptian ruler Nepherites I provided Agesilaus of Sparta with the equipment for 100 triremes, while his successor, Hakor, sent 50 triremes to the Cypriot rebel Evagoras in 381 BC. Just because the term 'trireme' is used in Greek texts describing the Egyptian navy in the late 4th century BC, this does not rule out the possibility that their fleets also included lighter vessels, such as the triakontors (single-banked galleys with thirty oarsmen) that are said to have made up nearly half of the Persian navy assembled against Egypt in 374 BC.

Greco-Phoenician war-galleys and Egyptian triremes

Probably because of the accumulation of a large fleet of Greco-Phoenician-style war-galleys, the commercially astute 26th-Dynasty Egyptian rulers were able temporarily to regain control of the Levantine sea-trade. But Egypt's declining military power was still primarily land-based and, although Egyptian shipwrights are documented in Babylon in the early 6th century BC, the Late Period fleet was evidently manned primarily by Phoenicians.

Excavations at Tell Defenna (ancient Daphnae) in northern Egypt, initially by Flinders Petrie (1886), and, more recently, by Mohamed Abd el-Maksoud (2009–15), have provided an intriguing view of the nature of permanent bases of such 26th-Dynasty Greco-Phoenician mercenary troops. The site is dominated by the surviving parts of a casemate mud-brick platform originally about 10 metres in height, and probably surmounted by a fort founded by Psamtek I. To the east of the fortifications was a contemporary civilian settlement, from which many Greek military artefacts of the 6th century BC were excavated, thus suggesting that it may perhaps have served as a naval base from which Greek-style war-galleys could be deployed.

According to the 5th-century BC Greek historian Herodotus (in Book II of his *History*), the military operations of the 26th-Dynasty pharaohs in the Near East were partly sea-borne, as they sought to keep the Babylonian and Persian empires at bay. Nekau II (*c.*610–595 BC), for instance, is said to have built a fleet of ramming war-galleys that may perhaps have been an early form of trireme. These boats are alleged to have been used both in the Mediterranean and the Red Sea, and it is possible that an abortive canal between the Nile Delta and the Red Sea (ascribed initially to Nekau and later to the Persian emperors) was intended to allow naval forces to be transferred from the Red Sea to the Mediterranean when required. A few years later, the pharaoh Apries (*c.*589–570) is said to have launched successful naval campaigns against Cyprus and Phoenicia, extensively utilizing the mercenary fleet.

Egypt's naval role in the Persian empire

In the 27th Dynasty (525–404 BC), when Egypt had become a satrapy in the Persian empire, its military capability was exploited for further Persian imperial expansion. Textual sources indicate, for example, that Egyptians were involved in the Persian naval assault on Miletus that effectively ended the Ionian revolt in 494 BC, and also that Egyptian military and naval resources contributed significantly to the wars fought by Darius and Xerxes on Greece in 490 and 480 BC. The fleet that Xerxes deployed against the mainland Greek states in 480/79 BC included two hundred Egyptian triremes led by Achaemenes, Xerxes's brother. In the battle of Artemisium, the Egyptian contingent are said to have captured five Greek ships along with their crews. That native Egyptian commanders, such as the well-known 'collaborator' Udjahorresnet, could achieve the rank of admiral in the Persian fleet during the 27th Dynasty, is probably a good indication of their quality.

There was a brief period of Egyptian independence in the first half of the 4th century BC (corresponding to the 28th–30th dynasties), and it was during this time that the 30th-Dynasty ruler Teos is said to have made the crucial appointment of an Athenian, Chabrias, as commander of his naval units in 361, when fending off an attempt at re-conquest of Egypt by the Persian emperor Artaxerxes II. There was therefore still clearly a considerable reliance on Greek expertise in naval warfare (although of course it should also be borne in mind that we are heavily reliant on Greek accounts of events at this time, which may well elaborate their own involvement). Whether the maritime skills were still Greek-influenced or not, the existence of genuinely effective naval units seems to have allowed the Egyptian rulers of the 30th Dynasty to wield considerable strategic and tactical power in the East Mediterranean region. During the struggle to regain independence a fascinating incident occurred, in 400 BC, when Tamos, a renegade Persian admiral (although with an oddly Egyptian sounding name) is said to have sought asylum in Egypt, along with his fleet, only to be murdered by an unnamed Egyptian ruler (probably Amyrtaios) in order to acquire his naval assets.

Eventually the Egyptians were reconquered, although this second period as a satrapy was to last for only about a decade. It is notable that naval power was once again crucial for both sides, both in terms of Egyptian resistance, under Nectanebo II, and Persian conquest. A favourite Persian strategy was to seek to shadow the deployment of their armies by simultaneously sending fleets of ships along their flanks, as Xerxes did in 480 BC in his invasion of Greece. It was therefore crucial for the Egyptians to come up with a response to Persian fleet movements in the Mediterranean as well as repelling forces entering the Delta from the Levant. The historical sources for the conflict therefore make frequent reference to naval matters, including, in 361/360 BC, the creation of a substantial fleet to operate alongside the army in a general revolt of the western provinces of the Persian empire.

CHAPTER 8

DIPLOMACY AND EMPIRE BUILDING IN THE BRONZE AGE

THIS CHAPTER FOCUSES PRIMARILY ON THE so-called Amarna Letters (*c.*1350 BC), comprising items of diplomatic correspondence between Egypt and the great powers in Western Asia (e.g. Babylonia and Assyria) and the vassal states of Syria-Palestine. They provide a fascinating picture of the relationship between Egypt and these Near Eastern states and cities. The possible disintegration of the Egyptian 'empire' during the reign of Akhenaten may be documented in increasingly desperate pleas for assistance from Syro-Palestinian cities under siege.

The Egyptian dominance in Western Asia lasted perhaps as long as 800 years, but throughout this period the various sources of evidence are often difficult to reconcile. The essential dilemma is encountered in assimilating the contemporary Egyptian descriptions of military campaigns and victories, which fall mostly within the realm of propaganda and bravado, with the more patchily surviving evidence of diplomatic activity. If it were not for the survival of the set of cuneiform letters between Egyptian and Western Asiatic rulers, found at Amarna in 1887–92, the study of the Egyptian involvement in Western Asia would be dominated far more by the language of warfare than that of diplomacy.

In the rest of the Ancient Near East there was a strong tradition of treaties, by which power blocs were built up and maintained. There were two basic types of treaty in the second and first millennia BC, distinguished by the Akkadian terms *riksu* (a parity treaty) and *adê* (essentially an oath of loyalty or vassal treaty). In Syria-Palestine these kinds of texts seem to have appeared at a particularly early date, probably a natural consequence of the profusion of local princes in the Levant who were constantly obliged to clarify their positions by means of vassal and parity relationships. It was inevitable that Egypt should eventually bolster its domination of the region by assuming a pre-eminent role in this diplomatic activity. The use of Akkadian and Babylonian dialects as the *lingua franca* of treaties and correspondence, however, suggests that Egypt was simply absorbed into an existing network of international diplomacy, the origins of which lay in Mesopotamia.

Egyptian 'foreign policy': a brief history

Throughout the Old and Middle Kingdoms, southern Syria-Palestine was regarded as part of the Egyptian sphere of influence, but it was not until the reign of the 12th-Dynasty ruler Senusret III (*c.*1870–1831 BC) that Egypt began to play the part of a true international power. With a new northern capital aggressively named Itj-tawy ('Seizing the Two Lands') established by Amenemhat I in the area of Lisht, the scene was set for a more vigorous foreign policy both in Nubia and Syria-Palestine. Regular envoys were sent to such Syrian city-states as Ugarit and Byblos, and there was an increase both in foreign trade and in the fortification of Egypt's northeastern frontier. The growing Egyptian influence on Syria-Palestine in the Middle Kingdom is indicated by the fact that the native rulers of Byblos were writing their names in Egyptian hieroglyphs and using the Egyptian title of ḥȝty-ʿ (provincial governor).

On the basis of surviving monumental texts (such as the Semna boundary stelae) and the construction and expansion of major fortresses in the Second Cataract region, Senusret III was clearly concerned with the subjugation of Nubia, but he seems to have fought one campaign in Retenu (Syria-Palestine), culminating in the capture of the city of Shechem. This incident is recorded on the stele from the tomb of Khusobek, a military official of Senusret III, at Abydos (discussed in Chapter 4). There is also a roughly contemporary stele found at the village of Mit Rahina (on the site of Memphis), which mentions booty from 'Asia'. This fragment of the royal annals (or '*gnwt*') of Amenemhat II (*c.*1911–1877 BC) shows that something approximating to the modern concept of a historical record (although lacking any analytical component) was already being compiled in the Middle Kingdom. The annals took the form of detailed records of the political and religious events from each year of the king's reign, including a great deal of information concerning military and trading expeditions to foreign countries. They suggest that Egypt had a range of different kinds of relations (both peaceful and aggressive) with the various parts of Western Asia, and that a number of treaties probably existed between Egypt and some individual Levantine cities. The north Syrian city of Tunip was clearly trading amicably with Egypt, but other Asiatic contacts seem to have been more bellicose. One section of the annals describes a small group of Egyptians entering 'bedouin' territory (probably a region of Sinai) to 'hack up the land', while two other military expeditions were launched against unknown walled towns. The defeated peoples were described as *Aamu* (Asiatics), and 1554 of them are said to have been captured; these significant numbers of foreign captives probably tie in directly with other textual evidence comprising extensive lists of Asiatic slaves working in Thebes in the later Middle Kingdom.

Further evidence for foreign relations at the time of Amenemhat II takes the form of the so-called 'Tod treasure', discovered in 1936 by François Bisson de la Roque, underneath a Middle Kingdom temple at the site of Tod, on the east bank of the Nile, south of Armant. This find comprised a hoard of precious materials buried in four bronze caskets, each bearing the cartouche of Amenemhat II. The contents included silver vessels (which may have been made in Crete, or perhaps somewhere in Cretan-influenced Western Asia), a silver lion, gold ingots, and lapis lazuli cylinder seals from Mesopotamia. Not only was this discovery one of the richest finds of silver in Egypt, but the evidence it provides concerning contacts with Greece and the Near East during the Middle Kingdom is a valuable indication of the wide extent of Egyptian commerce at this date. In addition, the discovery of statuary of Amenemhat II's daughters and officials at a number of sites in Syria-Palestine probably also indicates a steady growth of Egyptian influence in the Levant.

Whereas the evidence for Egyptian foreign relations in the Middle Kingdom and Second Intermediate Period is rather sparse, by the beginning of the New Kingdom copious textual and archaeological data were beginning to emerge. As early as the reign of Ahmose (*c.*1550–1525 BC) the Egyptians were evidently already laying the foundations of their Asiatic empire by campaigning in southern Retenu, but the crucial difference from their earlier forays into the Levant was the increasing use of diplomacy. The rapid construction of a framework of alliances and treaties took place alongside the adoption of Asiatic weaponry and methods of warfare.

Thutmose III's successors had varying degrees of success in maintaining the empire. By the reign of Amenhotep III – who only fought one campaign in Retenu, in the fifth year of his reign – the evolution of a strong mesh of diplomatic links seems to have allowed the emphasis to shift completely from battles to treaties. At a local level, the Egyptian garrisons in Syria-Palestine were able to police both the vassal cities and the troublesome bands of nomadic peoples such as the Shasu and Apiru. On a wider international level, treaties were drawn up, gifts traded, and royal sons and daughters given in marriage between the kings of Egypt, Mitanni, Assyria, Babylonia, Arzawa, Alashiya (Cyprus) and the Hittite empire. It is this golden age of ancient diplomacy that is documented in the archive of 'Amarna Letters', discovered in the capital city of Akhenaten (*c.*1352–1336 BC) at Amarna, as well as caches of similar cuneiform tablets found at the sites of Alalakh, Taanach and Boghazköy.

The Amarna Letters

An initial cache of clay cuneiform tablets was discovered in 1887 at the New Kingdom Egyptian city site of Amarna. Further illicit excavations led to the appearance of a number of clay cuneiform tablets on the antiquities market. The importance of these documents was not immediately recognized, and many passed into private hands, but Wallis Budge of the British Museum believed the tablets to be genuine and purchased a number of them. The tablets are now held primarily by the British Museum, the Egyptian Museum in Berlin, the Louvre, and the Egyptian Museum, Cairo.

There are 382 known tablets, more than half of which derive from the 'Place of the Letters of Pharaoh', a building identified as the official 'records office' in the central city at Amarna. Their exact chronology is still debated, but they span a few decades in the mid-14th century BC, beginning around year thirty of the reign of Amenhotep III (c.1360) and extending no later than the first year of Tutankhamun's reign (c.1336 BC), with the majority dating to the time of Akhenaten (1352–1336 BC). Most are written in the Babylonian dialect of the Akkadian language, which was the *lingua franca* of the time, although the languages of the Assyrians, Hittites and Hurrians (Mitanni) are also represented.

Couched in a great deal of Bronze Age diplomatic jargon, most of the Amarna tablets are letters sent from the princes of city-states in Syria-Palestine to the king of Egypt or his representative, the *rabisu*. About one fifth of them were sent by Ribaddi of Byblos, who is at one stage actually rebuked by the pharaoh for his obsession with letter-writing. A whole series of Ribaddi's letters appear to have been pleas for military assistance, including this desperate plea for help: 'May it seem right to the Lord, Sun of the Lands, to give me twenty teams of horses. Send help quickly to protect Sumura town. All the remaining garrison troops are having problems and there are only a few people in this city. If you fail to send any soldiers, there will be no city left at all'. Because the letters from vassals never include dates and rarely give the name of the sender or receiver, the problem of their correct chronological order has never been satisfactorily solved, although there are a few clues such as references to contemporary vassal-princes and the use of the pet name Mayati for the princess Meretaten.

Apart from these chronological uncertainties, the historical value of the Amarna Letters is reduced by the almost total absence of letters sent *by* the pharaoh (as opposed to letters received) and the fact that the archive probably dates only to a short period in the mid-14th century BC. The importance of the surviving correspondence, however, is that it conveys an impression of the unscrupulous diplomatic machinations and double-dealing during the New Kingdom, thus counterbalancing the relentless depiction of heroic victories and streams of tribute bearers presented on the walls of Egyptian temples. The letters also shed light on commerce throughout the Near East, providing information on the values of particular materials and commodities such as glass, gold and iron, while the various forms of address employed in the letters suggest the standing of the writers in relation to the Egyptian royal court. A small number of the letters (two labelled with dates in hieratic script) were sent from major foreign rulers such as Ashuruballit of Assyria, Burnaburiash of Babylon, and Tushratta of Mitanni to Amenhotep III and Akhenaten. The rulers address one another as 'brother' – as opposed to the terms 'father', 'sun' and 'god' used by vassal-princes to address the pharaoh – and send such messages as congratulations on accession to the throne, announcement of their own accession or complaints concerning the poor quality (or non-arrival) of gifts. The home territory of Egypt itself was not yet under threat from the other great powers, but the rulers of the various empires were keen to ensure that the Egyptian king did not develop too close an alliance with any of their rivals.

Clay cuneiform tablet (Amarna Letter 15), written in an Assyrian dialect of Akkadian, sent by the Assyrian ruler Ashuruballit to an Egyptian ruler (probably Akhenaten), c.1350 BC; it mentions a gift of a chariot and two horses. (New York: Metropolitan Museum of Art 24.2.11; photograph: MMA Open Content Program)

The letter from the Assyrian king Ashuruballit I (c.1365–1330 BC) appears to be the first one sent between Assyria and Egypt, since the Assyrian empire was at this stage in its infancy, although eventually it would briefly incorporate Egypt, under the rulers Esarhaddon and Ashurbanipal (c.671–660 BC). Unusually, the letter is written in an Assyrian dialect of Akkadian (whereas the vast majority were written in Babylonian). The text is relatively typical, beginning with a greeting and continuing with a reference to gifts sent with the missive:

> Say to the King of Egypt: thus Ashuruballit the King of Assyria. For you, your household, for your country. Up to now, my predecessors have not written; today I write to you.

I send you a beautiful chariot, two horses and one date-stone of genuine lapis lazuli, as your greeting gift. Do not delay the messenger whom I send to you for a visit. He should visit and then leave for here. He should see what you are like and what your country is like, and then leave for here.

One group that Syro-Palestinian vassals frequently mention in the Amarna Letters are Apiru, who seem to have been widespread across the Near East throughout the 2nd millennium BC. The first translations of the letters spelt the ethnonym as Hapiru or Habiru, leading Biblical scholars to suggest that these might be the first textual references to Hebrews, and some researchers have gone so far as to correlate references to Apiru attacks with the Biblical account of Joshua's invasion of Canaan. However, the term Apiru cannot be conclusively linked etymologically with Ibri (Hebrew), and it is not even clear whether Apiru refers to a specific ethnicity, a social group, or an economic category, with one commentator suggesting that the term essentially meant 'social banditry'.

The Amarna Letters are often considered to document the temporary disintegration of Egyptian control over the Levant during the reign of Akhenaten, who left few records of military campaigns and is therefore assumed to have neglected foreign policy in favour of religious and political reforms within Egypt itself. Some researchers, however, take the view that these documents simply happen to have survived from Akhenaten's reign, and that if similar archives from earlier or later in the New Kingdom had also survived, they might turn out to contain equally frantic requests for assistance from Syro-Palestinian cities under threat from rival powers, such as Mitanni and the Hittites. It could therefore be legitimately argued that our traditional view of there being a real Egyptian empire in Syria-Palestine is largely based on the Egyptians' own accounts of their battles and victories (although there are admittedly also the physical archaeological remains of several Egyptian garrisons and administrative posts throughout the region), and that the rather chaotic state of affairs documented in the Amarna Letters might have actually been the normal condition of the Egyptian sphere of influence in the Levant throughout the New Kingdom rather than being a temporary aberration.

CHAPTER 9

WHAT CAN WE REALLY KNOW ABOUT EGYPTIAN WARFARE?

Egyptian military history is clearly a vast and often well-documented area of study, and the preceding chapters have primarily provided an overview of the current state of knowledge, with occasional patches of more comprehensive discussion. We can study in some detail both the weapons and the physical remains of some of the soldiers themselves, often providing us with very intimate and tangible glimpses of the human realities of warfare in the Bronze Age and early Iron Age. Via the surviving images of tomb paintings and the panoramic campaign images on the walls of New Kingdom temples, we can also observe some spectacular aspects of the actual conflicts that took place, as well as the aftermath of battle, in the form of surrendering foes and the display of exotic booty, and treatment of human captives. We have even been able to hear the individual voices of the rulers of nations and city-states across the Near East, particularly in the form of the Amarna Letters, speaking to one another in the diplomatic language of time, against the background of shifting borders and transient alliances.

As the chapters above have shown, it is essential to see all of this evidence, however vivid or compelling, as raw data, that must be carefully dissected and interpreted according to their physical and cultural contexts. Nothing can be taken at face-value, particularly when we are dealing with images and texts, spinning narratives that often belong within the realm of iconography and extended metaphor, as opposed to the solid ground of reportage or history.

The battles of Megiddo and Qadesh almost certainly took place, but the pictorial and textual evocations of these two events are not so much documents as 'memorializations' of conflict – just because they include the names of real people and places does not prevent them from being poetry rather than prose. Nevertheless, our ability to look at the actual battle-scarred face of King Seqenenra Tao II, feel the heft and lethal edges of daggers and *khepesh* swords wielded by Egyptian warriors, and stand almost inside authentic intact chariots, provides a proximity to the physical reality of Egyptian warfare that compensates to some extent for the difficulties encountered in pinning down real historical details of specific battles and campaigns.

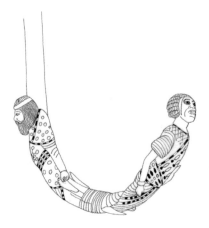

Handle of a ceremonial cane from the tomb of Tutankhamun, decorated with representations of an Asiatic and a Nubian, c.1330 BC.

SOURCES AND FURTHER READING

INTRODUCTION: GENERAL WORKS

Bestock, L. 2018. *Violence and Power in Ancient Egypt.* Oxford and New York.

Darnell, J. C. and Manassa, C. 2007. *Tutankhamun's Armies*, Hoboken NJ.

Hamblin, W. J. 2006. *Warfare in the Ancient Near East to 1600 BC.* New York.

Shaw, I. 1991. *Egyptian Warfare and Weapons.* Princes Risborough.

Shaw, I. 1996. Battle in ancient Egypt: the triumph of Horus or the cutting edge of the temple economy? In A. B. Lloyd (ed.), *Battle in Antiquity.* London, pp. 239–269.

Spalinger, A. J. 1982. *Aspects of the Military Documents of the Ancient Egyptians.* New Haven and London.

Spalinger, A. 2005. *War in Ancient Egypt.* Oxford.

1. INTERPRETING THE EVIDENCE FOR EGYPTIAN WARFARE

Baines, J. 1987. The stele of Khusobek: private and royal military narrative and values. In M. Görg (ed.), *Form und Mass.* Wiesbaden, pp. 43–61. [stele of Khusobek]

Bestock, L. *Violence and Power in Ancient Egypt.* pp. 27–33, 232–234. [paintings in Tomb 100 at Hierakonpolis; tombs of Iti-ibi and Iti-ibi-ikr]

Davis, W. 1992 *Masking the Blow: The Scene of Representation in Late Prehistoric Egyptian Art.* Berkeley, Los Angeles and London. [iconography of Protodynastic palettes]

Dreyer, G. 2000. Egypt's earliest historical event. *Egyptian Archaeology* 16: 6–7. [Narmer Label]

Fairservis, W.A. 1991. A revised view of the Na`rmr Palette. *Journal of the American Research Center in Egypt* 38: 1–20. [Narmer Palette]

Gaballa, G. A. 1976. *Narrative in Egyptian Art.* Mainz, pp. 39–40, 113–119. [Middle Kingdom tombs at Beni Hasan & the Battle of Qadesh]

Hall, E. S. 1986. *The Pharaoh Smites His Enemies.* Berlin. [royal smiting scenes]

Kanawati, N. and McFarlane, A. 1993. *Deshasha: The Tombs of Inti, Shedu and Others.* Sydney. [tomb of Inti at Deshasha]

el-Khadragy, M. 2006. The northern soldiers tomb at Asyut. *Studien zur Altägyptischen Kultur* 35: 147–165. [tomb of 'northern soldiers' at Asyut]

Lichtheim, M. 1976. *Ancient Egyptian Literature* II. Berkeley CA, pp. 11–15. [tomb of Ahmose son of Ibana]

Millet, N. B. 1990. The Narmer Macehead and related objects. *Journal of the American Research Center in Egypt* 27: 53–9. [interpretation of iconography of Protodynastic mace-heads and palettes]

Newberry, P. E. 1893. *Beni Hasan*, 2 vols. London. [Middle Kingdom tombs at Beni Hasan]

Quibell, J. E. and Hayter, A. G. K. 1927. *Excavations at Saqqara: Teti Pyramid, North Side.* Cairo. [Old Kingdom tombs at Saqqara]

Rizkana, I. and Seeher J. 1988. *Maadi* II. Mainz, pp. 51–52. [experimental use of maces]

Schele, L. and Miller, M. E. 1992. *The Blood of Kings: Dynasty and Ritual in Maya Art.* London.

Schulman, A. R. 1982. The battle scenes of the Middle Kingdom. *Journal of the Society for the Study of Egyptian Antiquities* 12: 165–83. [tomb of the general Intef]

Strudwick, N. 2006. *Masterpieces of Ancient Egypt.* London, pp. 34–35. [Battlefield Palette]

Vandersleyen, C. 1971. *Les guerres d'Amosis, fondateur de la XVIIIe dynastie.* Brussels, pp. 17–87. [tomb of Ahmose son of Ibana]

Vandier, J. 1950 *Mo'alla: La tombe d'Ankhtifi et la tombe de Sébekhotep.* Cairo. [tomb of Ankhtifi, the First Intermediate Period warlord]

2. FORTRESSES AND SIEGE WARFARE

Clarke, S. 1916. Ancient Egyptian frontier fortresses. *Journal of Egyptian Archaeology* 3: 155–79. [Egyptian fortresses in Nubia]

Dunham, D. 1967. *Second Cataract Forts II: Uronarti, Shalfak, Mirgissa.* Boston MA, pp. 141–176.

Eyre, C. 1990. The Semna stela: quotation, genre and functions of literature. In S. Israelit-Groll (ed.), *Studies in Egyptology presented to Miriam Lichtheim.* Jerusalem, Vol. 1, pp. 134–165. [Semna and Uronarti boundary stelae]

Gardiner, A. H. 1947. *Ancient Egyptian Onomastica.* Oxford, Vol. I, pp. 6–23, Pl. 2–2a. [the Ramesseum Onomasticon – list of fortresses' names]

Hasel, M. G. 1998. *Domination and Resistance: Egyptian Military Activity in the Southern Levant, 1300–1185BC.* Leiden. [the 'Ways of Horus' in northern Sinai and the Levant]

Heidorn, L. 2013. Dorginarti: fortress at the mouth of the rapids. In F. Jesse and C. Vogel (eds.), *The Power of Walls – Fortifications in Ancient Northeastern Africa.* Cologne, pp. 293–308. [Late Period fortress of Dorginarti]

Hoffmeier, J. K. and Maksoud, M. A. 2003. A new military site on 'The Ways of Horus': Tell el-Borg 1999–2001: a preliminary report. *Journal of Egyptian Archaeology* 89: 169–197 [Tjaru, Tell Hebua and Tell Borg fortresses]

Kraemer, B. and Liszka, K. 2016. Evidence for administration of Nubian fortresses in the late Middle Kingdom. *Journal of Egyptian History* 9/1: 1–66; 9/2: 151–208. [Semna Despatches]

Mumford, G. 2006. Tell Ras Budran (Site 345): Defining Egypt's eastern frontier and mining operations in South Sinai during the Late

Old Kingdom (Early EB IV/MB I). *Bulletin of the American Schools of Oriental Research* 342: 13–67. [Tell Ras Budran fortress]

Näser, C., Becker, P., Kossatz, K. & Khaleel Elawad Karrar, O. 2017. Shalfak Archaeological Mission (SAM): the 2017 field season. *Journal of Egyptian Archaeology* 103: 153–171. [Shalfak fortress]

O'Connor, D. 2014. *The Old Kingdom Town at Buhen*. London. [Old Kingdom Buhen]

Oren, E. D. 2006. The establishment of Egyptian imperial administration on the 'Ways of Horus': an archaeological perspective from north Sinai. In E. Czerny (ed.), *Timelines: Studies in Honour of Manfred Bietak*. Leuven, pp. 279–292. [summary of Eliezer Oren's excavations of sites along the Ways of Horus in Sinai and southern Levant]

Pritchard, J. B. 1969. *Ancient Near Eastern Texts Relating to the Old Testament*. Princeton, p. 293. [Assyrian siege and conquest of Memphis]

Ruby, J. W. 1964. Preliminary report of the University of California expedition to Dabenarti, 1963. *Kush* 12: 54–6. [Dabenarti fortress]

Schulman, A. R. 1964. Siege warfare in pharaonic Egypt. *Natural History Magazine* 73/3: 12–21.

Shaw, I. and Jameson, R. 1993. Amethyst mining in the Eastern Desert: a preliminary survey at Wadi el-Hudi. *Journal of Egyptian Archaeology* 79: 81–98. [Wadi el-Hudi fortress]

Smither, P. C. 1945. The Semnah Despatches. *Journal of Egyptian Archaeology* 31: 3–10. [Semna Despatches]

Snape, S. 2013. A stroll along the Corniche? Coastal routes between the Nile Delta and Cyrenaica in the Late Bronze Age. In H. Riemer and F. Forster (eds.), *Desert Road Archaeology in the Eastern Sahara*. Cologne, pp. 439–454. [Zawiyet Umm el-Rakham]

Spencer, N., Stevens, A. and Binder, M. 2014. *Amara West: Living in Egyptian Nubia*, London.

Vercoutter, J. 1970–76. *Mirgissa*, 3 vols. Paris and Lille. [Mirgissa fortress]

Vila, A. 1970. L'armement de la forteresse de Mirgissa-Iken. *Revue d'Egyptologie* 22: 171–99. [weapons at Mirgissa]

Vogel, C. 2010. *The Fortifications of Ancient Egypt, 3000–1780 BC*. Oxford and New York.

3. IMAGES AND NARRATIVES OF BATTLE IN THE NEW KINGDOM

Breasted, J. H. 1903. *The Battle of Kadesh, a Study in the Earliest Known Military Strategy*. Chicago IL. [Battle of Qadesh]

Desroches-Noblecourt, C. 1971. *Grand temple d'Abou Simbel: la bataille de Qadech*. Cairo. [Battle of Qadesh]

Finkelstein, I., Ussishkin, D. and Halpern, B. (eds.) 200–2006. *Megiddo III–IV*. Tel Aviv. [recent excavations of ancient Megiddo: Tell el-Mutesellim]

Gardiner, A. H. 1960. *The Kadesh Inscriptions of Ramesses II*. Oxford. [Battle of Qadesh]

Kuentz, C. 1928–34. *La bataille de Qadech*. Cairo. [Battle of Qadesh]

Murnane, W. 1990. *The Road to Kadesh: A Historical Interpretation of the Battle Reliefs of King Sety I at Karnak*. 2nd ed. Chicago, IL. [Seti I battle scenes at Karnak]

Parr, P. J. 2014. *Excavations at Tell Nebi Mend* I. Cambridge. [archaeology of Qadesh]

Redford, D. B. 1982. A Bronze Age itinerary in Transjordan (nos. 89–101 of Thutmose III's list of Asiatic toponyms. *Journal of the Society for the Study of Egyptian Antiquities* 12/2: 55–74. [pioneering attempt to reconcile the landscape of Syria-Palestine with the bare textual outlines of an Egyptian campaign in the reign of Thutmose III]

Schulman, A. R. 1979. Diplomatic marriage in the Egyptian New Kingdom. *Journal of Near Eastern Studies* 38: 177–193. [Context of the Hittite marriage stele at Abu Simbel]

<http://luxortimes.com/2018/05/3500-year-old-army-generals-tomb-discovered-by-egyptian-archaeologists/> [tomb of the general Iwrhya, Saqqara]

4. WHY DID WARS HAPPEN AND HOW WERE THEY EXPERIENCED?

Baines, J. The stele of Khusobek, pp. 43–61.

Bietak, M. 1974. Die Totesumstände des Pharaos Seqenenre (17. Dynastie). *Annalen des Naturhistorischen Museums Wien* 78: 29–52. [body of Seqenenra Tao II]

Faulkner, R. 1953. Egyptian military organization. *Journal of Egyptian Archaeology* 39: 32–47. [Egyptian military camp scenes]

Filer, 1992. Head injuries in Egypt and Nubia: a comparison of skulls from Giza and Kerma. *Journal of Egyptian Archaeology* 78: 281–285. [cranial injuries]

Hoffman, M. 1979. *Egypt before the Pharaohs: The Prehistoric Foundations of Egyptian Civilization*. New York, pp. 90–99, Tables V–IX. [Jebel Sahaba]

Kemp, B. J. 1978. Imperialism and empire in New Kingdom Egypt. In P. D. A. Garnsey and C. R. Whittaker (eds.), *Imperialism in the Ancient World*. Cambridge, pp.7–57. [Egyptian imperialism]

Strudwick, N. 2005. *Texts from the Pyramid Age*. Leiden, pp. 333–335. [inscription of Pepynakht and repatriation of a soldier's body]

Lichtheim, M. 1973–5. *Ancient Egyptian Literature*, vols I–II. Berkeley CA,
    Vol. I p. 20, Vol. II pp. 7–15, 172 [biography of Weni, *Be a
    Scribe* (Papyrus Lansing) & *Tale of Sinuhe*]

Lorton, D. 1974. Terminology related to the laws of warfare in Dynasty
    XVIII. *Journal of the American Research Center in Egypt* 11: 53–68.

Martin, G. T. 1991. *The Hidden Tombs of Memphis*. London, pp. 56–59.
    [military camp scenes]

Parkinson, R. B. 1991. *Voices from Ancient Egypt: An Anthology of Middle
    Kingdom Writings*. London: BMP, pp. 93–95. [stele of Intefiker
    & Semna Despatches]

Peet, T. E. 1914. *The Stela of Sebek-khu: The Earliest Record of an Egyptian
    Campaign in Asia*. Manchester. [Middle Kingdom stele of
    Khusobek]

Pritchard, J. B. 1969. *The Ancient Near East, Supplementary Texts and
    Pictures*. Princeton, p. 554. [Victory Stele of Kamose]

Redford, D. B. 1992. *Egypt, Canaan and Israel in Ancient Times*. Princeton.
    [p. 51: analysis of rationale for Egyptian warfare in the Levant;
    pp. 63–64: Egyptian policy of destruction]

Sanchez, G. M. 2003. Injuries in the battle of Kadesh. *KMT: A Modern
    Journal of Ancient Egypt* 14/1: 58–65.

Schulman, A. R. 1964. *Military Rank, Title and Organization in the
    Egyptian New Kingdom*. Berlin. [military camp scenes]

Spalinger, A. 1985. Notes on the reliefs of the battle of Qadesh. In H.
    Goedicke (ed.), *Perspectives on the Battle of Qadesh*. Baltimore
    MD, pp. 7–15. [military camp at Qadesh]

Vogel, C. 2003. Fallen heroes? Winlock's 'slain soldiers' reconsidered.
    Journal of Egyptian Archaeology 89: 239–245. [mass-grave at Deir
    el-Bahari]

Winlock, H. E. 1945. *The Slain Soldiers of Neb-Hepet-Re` Mentu-Hotpe*.
    New York. [mass-grave at Deir el-Bahari]

5. WEAPONRY AND TACTICS

Davies, W. V. 1987. *Catalogue of Egyptian Antiquities in the British Museum
    VII: Tools and Weapons I: Axes*. London. [axes]

Littauer, M. A. and Crouwel, J. H. 1979. *Wheeled Vehicles and Ridden
    Animals in the Ancient Near East*. Leiden and Cologne.
    [chariots]

Littauer, M. A. & Crouwel, J. H. 1985. *Chariots and Related Equipment
    from the Tomb of Tut`ankhamun*. Oxford.

McLeod, W. E. 1970. *Composite Bows from the Tomb of Tut`ankhamun*.
    Oxford.

McLeod, W. E. 1982. *Self Bows and Other Archery Tackle from the Tomb of
    Tut`ankhamun*. Oxford.

Moorey, P. R. S. 1986. The emergence of the light, horse-drawn chariot in the Near East, *c.*2000–1500 B.C. *World Archaeology* 18/2: 196–215.

Parkinson, R. 1997. *The Tale of Sinuhe and Other Ancient Egyptian Poems.* Oxford.

Raulwing, P. and Clutton-Brock, J. 2009. The Buhen horse: fifty years after its discovery (1958–2008). *Journal of Egyptian History* 2/1: 1–106. [Buhen horse skeleton]

Shaw, I. 2001. Egyptians, Hyksos and military technology: causes, effects or catalysts? In A. J. Shortland (ed.), *The Social Context of Technological Change: Egypt and the Near East, 1650–1550 BC.* Oxford, pp. 59–72. [innovations in New Kingdom weaponry]

Veldmeijer, A. and Ikram, S. (eds.) 2013. *Chasing Chariots.* Leiden. [edited volume on many different aspects of Egyptian military use of chariots]

Veldmeijer, A., Ikram, S. and Skinner, L. 2018. *Chariots in Ancient Egypt: The Tano Chariot, a Case Study.* Leiden. [the Tano Chariot]

Vogel, C. 2013. Icon of propaganda and lethal weapon: further remarks on the late Bronze Age sickle sword. In S. O'Brien and D. Boatright (eds.), *Warfare and Society in the Ancient Eastern Mediterranean.* Oxford, pp. 71–87. [*khepesh* swords]

Wernick, N. E. 2004. A *khepesh* sword in the University of Liverpool Museum. *Journal of the Society for the Study of Egyptian Antiquities* 31: 151–155. [Liverpool *khepesh* sword]

Western, A. C. 1973. A wheel hub from the tomb of Amenhotep II. *Journal of Egyptian Archaeology* 59: 91–94. [chariots]

Western, A. C. & McLeod, W. 1995, Woods used in Egyptian bows and arrows. *Journal of Egyptian Archaeology* 81: 77–94.

6. CULTURE, ETHNICITY AND MOBILITY OF SOLDIERS AND WEAPONS

Cavillier, G. 2010. Shardana project – perspectives and researches on the Sherden in Egypt and Mediterranean. In *Syria* 87: 339–345. [the Sherden mercenaries]

Fischer, H. G. 1961. The Nubian Mercenaries of Gebelein during the First Intermediate Period. In *Kush* 9: 44–80.

Goedicke, H. (ed.) 1985. *Perspectives on the Battle of Kadesh*, Baltimore MD. [tactics]

Liszka, K. 2011. 'We have come from the Well of Ibhet': ethnogenesis of the Medjay. *Journal of Egyptian History* 4: 149–171. [the Medjay Nubians and Papyrus Boulaq 18]

Moorey, P. R. S. 1989. The Hurrians, the Mitanni and technological innovation. In L. de Meyer and E. Haerinck (eds.), *Archaeologica Iranica and Orientalis*. Ghent, pp. 273–286. [transfer of military technology from Mitanni to Egypt]

Moorey, P. R. S. 2001. The mobility of artisans and opportunities for technology transfer. In A. J. Shortland (ed.), *The Social Context of Technological Change: Egypt and the Near East, 1650–1550 BC*. Oxford, pp. 1–14. [transfer of chariotry technology]

O'Connor, D. 1990. The nature of Tjemhu (Libyan) society in the later New Kingdom. In A. Leahy (ed.), *Libya and Egypt c1300–750 B.C.* London, pp. 29–114. [Libyan ethnicities]

Pusch, E. 1996. 'Pi-Ramesses-beloved-of-Amun, headquarters of their chariotry': Egyptians and Hittites in the Delta residence of the Ramessides. In A. Eggebrecht (ed.), *Pelizaeus Museum Hildesheim: the Egyptian Collection*. Mainz, pp. 126–145. [Hittite weaponry at Piramesse/Qantir]

Pusch, E. B. and Jakob, S. 2003. Der Zipfel des diplomatischen Archivs Ramses' II. *Ägypten & Levante* 13: 143–153. [fragment of a cuneiform tablet from Piramesse/Qantir]

Quirke, S. 2004. *Egyptian Literature 1800 BC: Questions and Readings*. London, pp. 112–120. [*The Instruction Addressed to King Merikara*]

Schofield, L. and Parkinson, R. 1994. Of helmets and heretics: a possible Egyptian representation of Mycenaean warriors on a papyrus from el-Amarna. *Annual of the British School at Athens* 89: 157–70. [Mycenaean soldiers on Amarna papyrus]

Schulman, A. 1988. Hittites, helmets and Amarna: Akhenaten's first Hittite war. In D. Redford (ed.), *Akhenaten Temple Project II*. Toronto, pp. 54–79. [Egyptian images of Hittites]

Snape, S. R. 2003. The emergence of Libya on the horizon of Egypt. In D. O'Connor & S. Quirke (eds.), *Mysterious Lands*. London, pp. 93–106. [Meshwesh & Libu – archaeology and texts]

Wainwright, G. A. 1962. The Meshwesh. *Journal of Egyptian Archaeology* 48: 89–99.

7. NAVAL BATTLES

Bénédite, G. 1916. Le couteau de Gebel el-'Arak, Étude sur un nouvelle objet préhistorique acquis par le musée du Louvre, *Fondation Eugène Piot, Monuments et mémoires* 22: 1–34. [primary publication of the Gebel el-Arak knife-handle]

Cifola, B. 1994. The role of the Sea Peoples at the end of the Late Bronze Age: a reassessment of textual and archaeological evidence. *Orientis antiqui miscellanea / Istituto per l'Oriente C. A. Nallino* 1: 1–23.

Delange, É. 2009. Le poignard *égyptien* dit "du Gebel el-Arak", Paris.

Dothan, T. K. and Dothan, M. 1992. *People of the Sea: The Search for the Philistines*, New York.

Harrison, T. P. (ed.) 2008. *Cyprus, the Sea Peoples and the Eastern Mediterranean: Regional Perspectives of Continuity and Change*. Toronto.

Killebrew, A. E. and Lehmann G. (eds.), 2013. *The Philistines and Other "Sea Peoples" in Text and Archaeology*. Atlanta, GA.

Lloyd, A. B. 1972. Triremes and the Saïte navy. *Journal of Egyptian Archaeology* 58: 268–279.

Oren, E. D. (ed.), 2000. *The Sea Peoples and Their World: A Reassessment*, Philadelphia, PA.

Raban, A. 1989. The Medinet Habu ships: another interpretation. *International Journal of Nautical Archaeology and Underwater Exploration* 18/2: 163–171.

Sandars, N. K. 1985. *The Sea Peoples: Warriors of the Ancient Mediterranean 1250–1150 B.C.* 2nd ed. London and New York.

Shaw, I. 1996. Gebel el-Arak. *The Grove Dictionary of Art*, ed. J. Shoaf-Turner. London.

Wachsmann, S. 1981. The ships of the Sea Peoples. *International Journal of Nautical Archaeology* 10: 187–220.

Wachsmann, S. 2013. *The Gurob Ship-cart Model and its Mediterranean Context*. Texas. [Gurob ship model]

Ward, C. & Zazzaro, C. 2010. Evidence for pharaonic seagoing ships at Mersa/ Wadi Gawasis, Egypt. *International Journal of Nautical Archaeology* 39: 27–43. [Mersa Gawasis boats]

Zangani, F. 2016. Amarna and Uluburun: reconsidering patterns of exchange in the Late Bronze Age. *Palestine Exploration Quarterly* 148/4: 230-244. [the Ulu Burun shipwreck in the context of the Amarna Letters]

8. DIPLOMACY AND EMPIRE BUILDING IN THE BRONZE AGE

Cohen, R. and Westerbrook, R. (eds.) 2000. *Amarna Diplomacy: The Beginnings of International Relations*. London and Baltimore.

Farag, S. 1980. Une inscription memphite de la XII dynastie. *Revue d'Egyptologie* 32: 75–82. [Middle Kingdom diplomacy and empire building]

Marcus, E. 2007. Amenemhet II and the sea: maritime aspects of the Mit Rahina (Memphis) Inscription. *Ägypten & Levante* 17: 137–190. [Amenemhat II's foreign relations]

Moran, W. L. 1992. *The Amarna Letters*. London and Baltimore.

Pierrat-Bonnefois, G. 2008. The Tod Treasure. In J. Aruz, K. Benzel and J. M. Evans (eds.), *Beyond Babylon: Art, Trade and Diplomacy in the Second Millennium BC*. New York, pp. 65–68.

Weeks, N. 2004. *Admonition and Curse: The Ancient Near Eastern Treaty/ Covenant Form as a Problem in Inter-Cultural Relationships*. London. [*riksu* and *adê* treaties]

ACKNOWLEDGEMENTS

I am grateful to my amazing wife, colleague and frequent co-worker on Egyptian field projects, Dr Elizabeth Bloxam, for countless stimulating discussions about Egyptian culture and archaeology over the years. I am also grateful to Paul Vyse for his excellent work on several of the line drawings.

INDEX